EXECUTIVE EDITORS
Mike Mifsud, Alan Doan, Jenny Doan,
Sarah Galbraith, David Mifsud

MANAGING EDITOR
Natalie Earnheart

CREATIVE DIRECTOR
Christine Ricks

PHOTOGRAPHY TEAM
Mike Brunner, Lauren Dorton, Jennifer Dowling,
Dustin Weant

PATTERN TEAM
Edie McGinnis, Denise Lane, Jessica Toye, Tyler MacBeth

PROJECT DESIGN TEAM
Jenny Doan, Natalie Earnheart

EDITOR & COPYWRITERS
Camille Maddox, Nichole Spravzoff, David Litherland,
Julie Barber

SEWIST TEAM
Jenny Doan, Natalie Earnheart, Carol Henderson,
Janice Richardson

QUILTING & BINDING DEPARTMENT
Becky Bowen, Glenda Rorabough, Nikki LaPiana, Amy Turpin,
Debbie Elder, Holly Clevenger, Kristen Cash, Todd Harman,
Jessica Paup, Jan Meek, Linda Frump, Franny Fleming, Rachael
Joyce, Selena Smiley, Nora Clutter, Lyndia Lovell, Jackie Jones,
Roxanna Hinkle, Deloris Burnett, Bernice Kelley, Darlene Smith,
Janet Yamamoto

LOCATION CREDIT
Ryan and Dakota Redford
Home Inn Hamilton
Hotel Hamilton
Roger and Julie Hill, Hamilton, MO
David Prather, Hamilton Middle School

PRINTING COORDINATORS
Rob Stoebener, Seann Dwyer

PRINTING SERVICES
Walsworth Print Group
803 South Missouri
Marceline, MO 64658

CONTACT US
Missouri Star Quilt Company
114 N Davis
Hamilton, MO 64644
888-571-1122
info@missouriquiltco.com

content

Oops! Sometimes we make mistakes. To find corrections to every issue of Block go to: www.msqc.co/corrections

hello

I love finding opportunities to celebrate. Just about every day of the year has a reason and sometimes I even make up my own little holidays! During April alone you'll find everything from April Fool's Day on the first of the month to Sibling's Day on the 10th, Barbershop Quartet Day on the 11th, Scrabble Day on the 13th, Jelly Bean Day on the 22nd, and Pretzel Day on the 26th, all the way to Zipper Day on the 29th!

In fact, this entire year is a reason to celebrate because Missouri Star just turned 10 back in September. It's been a wonderful journey to this incredible milestone with plenty of interesting stops along the way. All these milestones, large and small, brighten up our days and give us a reason to stop and consider how truly blessed we are. That's what celebrations are all about, recognizing growth and expressing gratitude.

Family and friends make the tough times worth it and seeing what we can accomplish together is one of my greatest joys. I've said it before, and I'll definitely say it again: life doesn't turn out the way you think it will. Expect to be surprised! I hope you enjoy this issue of Block. It's been so much fun hearing all these stories from loved ones who have reached important milestones and shared them with us. Thank you for sharing your quilting journey with us. We're so glad to be a part of it.

Jenny

JENNY DOAN
MISSOURI STAR QUILT CO

For the tutorial and everything you need to make this quilt visit:

www.msqc.co/celebrationblock19

rose garden

Birthdays are always a big deal in my house, and with seven children, I make sure each child's birthday is extra special. From their favorite-colored balloons to a cake with matching frosting and a candle for each year, you can imagine how many candles adorn their cakes now! I'll never stop doing my best to make their day special, just like my friend June and her mother.

If there was one day June looked forward to more than Christmas, it was her birthday! Like all kids growing up, she loved the one day of the year that was entirely hers. And just like other kids, June loved all the birthday festivities: Blowing out candles on a big cake topped with her name and mouth-watering frosting roses, tearing into presents wrapped in glossy, colorful paper, and spending the rest of the day sharing her new toys with her friends. But what June loved most of all was the one thing that made her birthday parties different.

Practically every birthday party has balloons, but June had never been to a party that had as many as hers. On the morning of her birthday, she would get up early and tiptoe down the stairs to sneak a peek at her birthday decorations. The sight would always bring a big grin to June's face; balloons were everywhere, in every color of the rainbow! June's mother made sure every room was colorful and crowded with as many balloons as she could fit. She would tie them to every chair, to the coffee table, the cabinet handles, even the dog had a balloon tied to his tail!

When there was nothing left to tether a balloon to, June's mother would let the rest float freely around the house.

As soon as June's friends arrived, they would all skip through the forest of balloon strings dangling from the ceiling, giggling as the strings tickled their faces. June and her friends would grab handfuls of strings, give a strong tug and watch them float slowly back up to the ceiling. Then, after all the presents were unwrapped and June and her friends were coming down from their frosting-fueled sugar rushes, they would have even more fun.

The Wizard of Oz was one of June's favorite movies, not just because of Dorothy's sparkly slippers or her cute dog Toto. She loved the Munchkins, and their sweet, squeaky voices! June's mother would bring a balloon down from the ceiling, puncture a tiny hole by the knot, inhale a big gulp of helium, and send June and her friends into a laughing fit as she sang "The Lollipop Guild" in her squeaky Munchkin voice.

After June's mother had sang all the songs she could, she told the kids to grab some balloons and follow her outside. June loved this part of her birthday, it was another little tradition her mother upheld every single year. She and her friends would stand together with their balloon bouquets bumping into each other until her mother told them to release them. "All together now, kids. 1 ... 2 ... 3 ... Let go!" They released their balloons and watched them float lazily into the blue sky. June and her friends would stay and watch their balloons drift away, getting smaller and smaller the higher they floated. She held her mother's hand, smiling up at the colorful dots scattered across the sky.

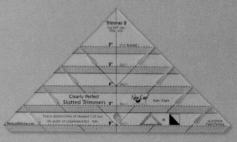

materials

QUILT SIZE
67½" x 67½"

BLOCK SIZE
4½" finished

QUILT TOP
2 packages of 5" print squares
1½ yards of pink fabric
1¼ yards of white fabric

BORDER
1¼ yards

BINDING
¾ yard

BACKING
4¼ yards - vertical seam(s)

OTHER SUPPLIES
Clearly Perfect Slotted Trimmer B

SAMPLE QUILT
Best Friends Forever by Stacy Iest
Hsu for Moda Fabrics

1 cut

From the pink fabric, cut:

- (6) 5½" strips across the width of the fabric – subcut each strip into 5½" squares. Each strip will yield 7 squares and a **total of 36** are needed. Set aside 6 squares for another project.

- (6) 3" strips across the width of the fabric – subcut the strips into 3" x 6" rectangles. Each strip will yield 6 rectangles and a **total of 32** are needed. Set aside 4 rectangles for another project.

From the white fabric, cut:

- (6) 5½" strips across the width of the fabric – subcut each strip into 5½" squares. Each strip will yield 7 squares and a **total of 36** are needed. Set aside 6 squares for another project.

- (2) 5" strips across the width of the fabric – subcut each strip into 5" squares. Each strip will yield 8 squares and a **total of 16** are needed.

2A

From the border fabric, cut:

- (7) 5" strips across the width of the fabric – subcut (1) 5" square from 1 strip. Add the square to the 5" print squares. Add the remainder of the strip to the 6 strips you've just cut and set aside until you're ready to make the border.

2 make half-square triangles

On the reverse side of the 36 white 5½" squares, draw a line from corner to corner once on the diagonal. Layer a marked white square with a pink square with right sides facing. Sew on both sides of the drawn line using a scant ¼" seam allowance. Cut on the drawn line. **2A**

Before opening and pressing each unit, trim each to 5" using Piece B of the Clearly Perfect Slotted Trimmer. While trimming the unit to size, use the slots to knock off the dog ears. **2B**

Open and press the seam allowance toward the dark fabric. You should have (72) 5" unfinished half-square triangles. **2C**

3 make star leg units

Pick up the 5" white squares and the 3" x 6" pink rectangles.

Fold the white squares in half and finger press a crease on one side of the square. Place a pink rectangle atop a white square on an angle with right sides facing. Be sure the rectangle crosses over the upper corner as well as the finger-pressed crease by about ¼". Sew in place. Press the rectangle over the seam allowance. Repeat for the other side of the square. **Note:** you want the seam to fall within ¼" of the edge of the square so you don't lose the points. **3A 3B 3C 3D**

Turn the square over so the reverse side is up. Trim all excess fabric away evenly with the edges of the square. **Make 16. 3E 3F**

4 arrange and sew

Lay out the 5" squares, half-square triangle units, and star leg blocks in rows. Each row is made up of **13 blocks** and **13 rows** are needed.

Row A begins and ends with a 5" print square and each square alternates with a half-square triangle unit. Make 6 rows in this manner and press all the seam allowances toward the left. **4A**

Row B begins and ends with a half-square triangle unit and alternates with a 5" square. A star leg unit replaces the half-square triangle that would be in the

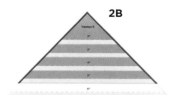

2B

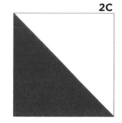

2C

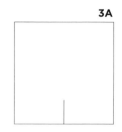

3A

3B

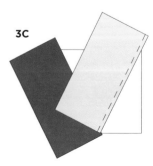

3C

center of the strip. Make 6 rows in this manner and press all seam allowances toward the right. **4B**

Row C begins and ends with a 5″ square and each square alternates with a star leg unit. Be aware of the direction the star leg is pointing. Make 1 row like this and press the seam allowances toward the left. **4C**

Lay out the rows beginning with a Row A and alternate with a Row B. Row C is the 7th row. After Row C is in place, add a Row B. Continue to alternate Rows A and B until all the rows are laid out. Sew the rows together to complete the center of the quilt. Refer to the diagram on page 15, if necessary.

5 border

Pick up the 5″ strips that were set aside for the border earlier. Sew the strips together end-to-end to make one long strip. Trim the borders from this strip.

3D

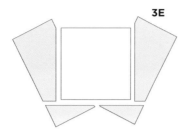

3E

3F

Notice there is a star leg unit used in each side border as well as the top and bottom. Measure the quilt top beginning with the sixth row and go toward the top. After adding ¼″ for the needed seam allowance, your measurement should be approximately 27½″. Cut 2 pieces to your measurement for each side of the quilt.

Sew a 5″ x <u>your measurement</u> strip to either side of a star leg unit. Make sure the star leg is oriented in the correct direction. Make 2 and sew one to each side of the quilt top. **5A**

Measure the quilt top beginning with the sixth vertical row and go toward either edge. After adding ¼″ for the needed seam allowance, your measurement should be approximately 32″. Cut 2 pieces to your measurement for each side of the block.

Sew a 5″ x <u>your measurement</u> strip to either side of a star leg unit. Make sure the star leg is oriented in the correct direction. Make 2 and sew one to the top of the quilt and one to the bottom. **5B**

5A

4A

4B

4C

5B

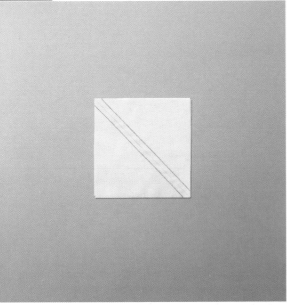

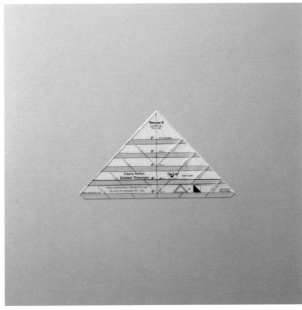

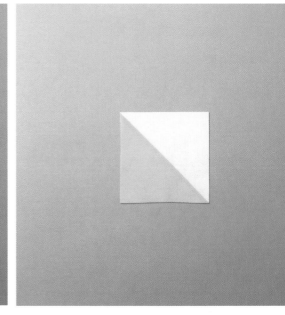

1 On the reverse side of each white 5½" square, draw a line from corner to corner once on the diagonal. Layer a marked white square with a pink square with right sides facing. Sew on both sides of the drawn line.

2 After cutting on the drawn line, trim each half-square triangle unit to 5" using Piece B of the Clearly Perfect Slotted Trimmer.

3 Open each half-square triangle unit and press the seam allowance toward the dark fabric.

4 Place a 3" x 6" rectangle on a 5" white square with right sides facing on an angle, making sure the seam allowance crosses over the center of the square. Sew in place, press the rectangle over the seam allowance. Repeat for the other side of the square.

5 Press the rectangle over the seam allowance toward the outside of the white square. Turn the square over and trim all excess fabric away evenly with the edges of the square.

6 Make 16 star leg units.

6 quilt and bind

Layer the quilt with batting and backing and quilt. After the quilting is complete, square up the quilt and trim away all excess batting and backing. Add binding to complete the quilt. See Construction Basics (pg. 118) for binding instructions.

diamond dance

If you're a holiday baby, I sure hope you feel adored on your special day. Because whether you were born on Valentine's Day, Halloween, or even Tax Day, you deserve to be celebrated! My young friend, Tyler, was born on the 4th of July. Here's his story.

Independence Day was the best day of the year for young Tyler Stewart. Every moment from dawn to dusk was filled with Fourth of July fun and, to top it all off, it was his birthday, too!

The day started early, just like every year. Mom filled the cooler with egg salad sandwiches, sliced watermelon, and bottles of strawberry lemonade. Dad loaded the picnic quilt and a big beach umbrella into the back of the pickup. Tyler dressed in his #4 little league baseball uniform. Then, it was off to the parade.

As the very last row of parade ponies pranced down the road, Tyler took off to the far edge of the park where the baseball diamond stood. It was time for the all-star game, and Tyler played first base.

By the time he was 11 years old, Tyler had played in four different Fourth of July all-star games. It seemed four was his lucky number. And on this particular Fourth of July, Tyler was placed fourth in the batting lineup. When he got to home plate, the bases were loaded. The pitcher tossed the ball and Tyler swung with all his might. *Crack!* That ball went soaring over the outfield, landing with a "*plop*" in the pond just beyond the fence!

And just like that, #4 Tyler Stewart brought in four runs during his fourth all-star game on his Fourth of July

birthday. That year, more than any other, it sure felt like the firework show was put on just for him!

Tyler's holiday birthday was almost magical, but what's it like for other folks? We asked the holiday babies here at Missouri Star. Here are a few of their answers:

April Sweetland's birthday is April Fool's Day—that's how she got her cute name! And because it's her special day, no one ever played jokes on her. Pretty sweet deal!

Trisa Gydesen was born on Thanksgiving Day. In fact, she was nearly born at the Thanksgiving dinner table! Her mother refused to go to the hospital for fear of missing Grandma's Waldorf salad!

Camille Maddox's son was born six days before Christmas. To make the day special, she always replaces stockings and Christmas greenery with a "Happy Birthday" banner and balloons. The next day, the Christmas decorations go back up on the mantle.

Annette Ashbach's daughter was born on Leap Day, February 29th—a day that only occurs every four years. "When February 28 arrived, we would tell her, 'Tomorrow is your birthday!" The next day, on March 1st, we'd say, 'Yesterday was your birthday' She didn't think that was funny. On her 20th year (which was her fifth actual birthday) we pulled out all the stops with coloring books, crayons, a Barbie doll, and a beautiful doll cake with a piped frosting gown. It was the perfect birthday for a five year old!

the tutorial and everything
you need to make this quilt visit:
www.msqc.co/celebrateblock19

materials

QUILT SIZE
90" x 88"

BLOCK SIZE
4⅛" x 9½" finished

QUILT TOP
1 package 10" print fabric
3 yards background squares - includes inner border
1½ yards complementary fabric

OUTER BORDER
1½ yards

BINDING
¾ yard

BACKING
8 yards - vertical seam(s) or 2¾ yards
of 108" wide

OTHER SUPPLIES
Missouri Star 10" Half-Hexagon Template
Missouri Star Large Rhombus Template

SAMPLE QUILT
Seventh Inning Stretch by Jennifer Pugh
for Wilmington Prints

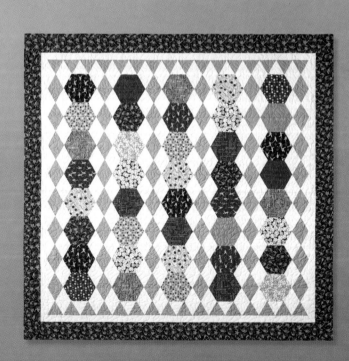

1 cut

From the background fabric, cut:

- (18) 4⅝" strips across the width of the fabric – subcut each strip into 60° triangles using the 10" Rhombus template. Each strip will yield 13 triangles and a **total of 226** are needed.

Note: on the template you will notice instructions saying, "Use this side for triangles." Instead, for this quilt, we are going to use the other side of the template that has the Missouri Star logo on it when cutting the triangles. Align the narrow, squared-off end of the template with the top of each strip (there will be ⅛" of fabric showing below the line drawn across the widest portion of the template) and cut the triangles. Turn the template 180° with each cut. Set aside the remainder of the fabric for the inner border.

From the complementary fabric, cut:

- (10) 4⅝" strips across the width of the fabric – subcut each strip into 60° triangles using the 10" Rhombus template. Each strip will yield 13 triangles and a **total of 128** are

needed. See **Note** about positioning the template.

From each 10" square, cut:

- 2 half-hexagons using the template. Fold each square in half, then place the template on a folded square and cut around the shape. Each square will yield 2 half-hexagons and a **total of 80** are needed. Keep all matching prints together. Set aside the remaining 2 squares for another project.

2 make 60° triangle units

Sew a background triangle to either side of a complementary triangle. Make 96 triangle units.

2A 2B 2C 2D

3 arrange and sew

Lay out the quilt row by row. Begin and end each row with a triangle unit and alternate the triangle units with a half-hexagon. Notice how the pieces are offset by ¼" as you align the 2 together. **3A 3B**

Be sure to match up the half-hexagons made from the same prints from 1 row

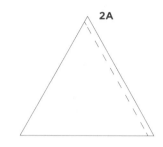

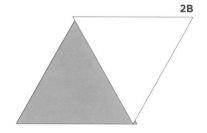

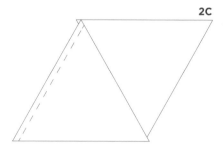

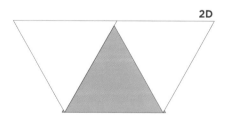

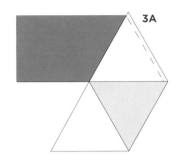

3A

3B

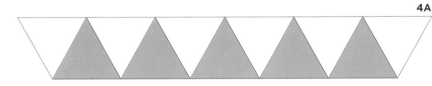

4A

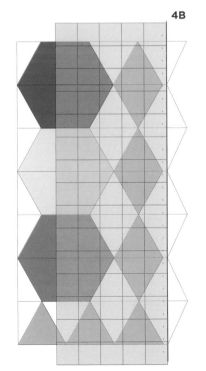

4B

to the next, so a complete hexagon is formed. Each row is made up of 6 triangle units and 5 half-hexagons and you need a **total of 16** rows. See the diagram on page 23 and notice that the even rows mirror the odd rows. Press the seam allowances in the odd rows toward the right and the even rows toward the left to make the seams nest.

After you have made all the rows and are satisfied with the layout, sew the rows together.

4 top and bottom pieced border

To make the top and bottom pieced border, sew together 33 triangles (17 background and 16 complementary) using a ¼″ seam allowance. Begin and end with a background triangle and alternate each background triangle with a complementary triangle. Make 2 and sew one to the top of the quilt and one to the bottom of the quilt. **4A**

Before adding the inner border, the sides must be squared up. Align the ¼″ mark on the ruler with the outside edge of the complementary triangles, then trim. You must leave a ¼″ seam allowance to avoid losing the points on the edge. **4B**

5 inner border

Cut (8) 2½″ strips across the width of the fabric. Sew the strips together end-to-end to make one long strip. Trim the borders from this strip.

Refer to Borders (pg. 118) in the Construction Basics to measure and cut the inner borders. The strips are approximately 74¾″ for the sides and approximately 80½″ for the top and bottom.

6 outer border

Cut (9) 5½″ strips across the width of the fabric. Sew the strips together end-to-end to make one long strip. Trim the borders from this strip.

Refer to Borders (pg. 118) in the Construction Basics to measure and cut the outer borders. The strips are

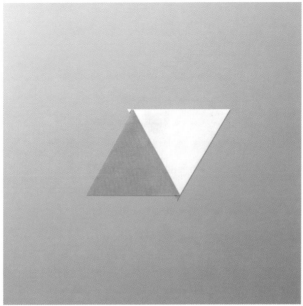

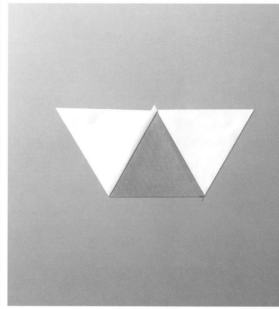

1 Sew a background triangle to a complementary triangle, offsetting the corners by ¼".

2 Open and press the seam allowance toward the dark fabric.

3 Add another white triangle to the other side of the complementary triangle. Press the seam allowance toward the dark fabric.

4 Alternate the triangle units with a print half-hexagon. Notice the pieces are offset by ¼" as you align them with right sides facing.

5 After sewing the half-hexagon to the triangle units, open and press the seam allowance toward the dark fabric.

6 Square up the sides of the quilt by aligning the ¼" mark of the ruler with the outside edge of the complementary triangles, trim.

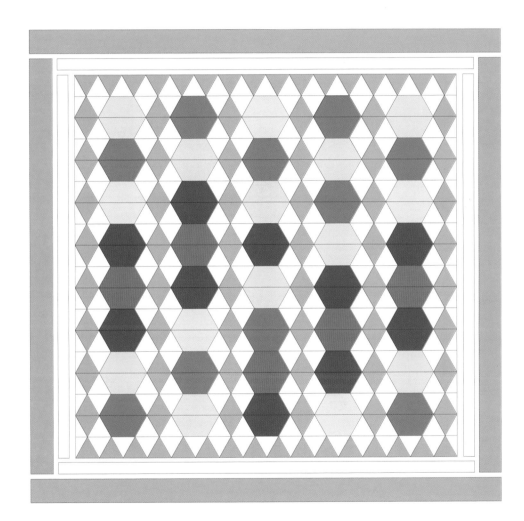

approximately 78¾" for the sides and approximately 90½" for the top and bottom.

7 quilt and bind

Layer the quilt with batting and backing and quilt. After the quilting is complete, square up the quilt and trim away all excess batting and backing. Add binding to complete the quilt. See Construction Basics (pg. 118) for binding instructions.

t-shirt quilt

T-shirts are the staples of our wardrobe, perhaps the most basic item we own. We don't put a lot of thought into them; they pile up in our drawers and get worn and reworn until they're stretched out, faded, and holey, but even then, we still love them. T-shirts get shot out of cannons at sporting events and given away at malls and grocery stores. They're not necessarily glamorous, but they're definitely comfortable, and we couldn't live without them!

The word T-shirt came about because of the actual shape of the garment. It's literally shaped like the uppercase letter "T." It was originally worn as an undergarment, especially for factory and farm workers who had tough, dirty jobs to do and needed something easy to wear and easy to clean. But, T-shirts soon took on a life of their own. They were part of the United States Navy uniform, which required a buttonless, cotton undershirt. Then, they became popular with bachelors who didn't know how to replace buttons. At first, it was actually controversial to wear T-shirts without a button up shirt over them, but Hollywood caused a stir when Marlon Brando wore an unadorned T-shirt in *A Streetcar Named Desire*. James Dean also wore white T-shirts with a casual flair that made him a fashion icon.

When you look at a stack of old T-shirts, what do you see? I see memories. I remember wearing one at a family reunion or at a football game. I think of a child off at college while fondly wearing a T-shirt from their alma mater and I can't help but snag a T-shirt when I'm at a concert! I've gathered up so many T-shirts from events, retreats, and travel, that my dresser can hardly contain them! So, what can they become? I hate to think of cutting them up for cleaning rags. Before you KonMari them into the Goodwill bag, consider a new use for your beloved T-shirts. We think this idea will definitely spark some joy!

T-shirt quilts make incredibly thoughtful gifts. They're perfect for practically any occasion and highly customizable. The design can be simple or complex, but the end result is always snuggly! Think about a loved one who has a formidable T-shirt stash and ask them if you can help reduce the bulk by making them a personalized quilt for their birthday, anniversary, graduation, or retirement.

Quilts are a special way to show you care! Maybe you have a beloved friend you love going to quilting retreats with. Take all those T-shirts you've gathered up over the years and surprise her with a quilt she'll adore. If you have children going off to college, collect all their high school T-shirts and stitch them up into quilts they'll cherish in their tiny dorm rooms. It's sure to make them feel more at home. Have fun and let those T-shirts keep making memories for years to come!

For the tutorial and everything
you need to make this quilt visit:
www.msqc.co/celebrateblock19

25

materials

QUILT SIZE
68½" x 83"

BLOCK SIZE
12" finished

QUILT TOP
20 T-shirts
1½ yards white fabric – includes inner border
½ yard print fabric

OUTER BORDER
1¼ yards

BINDING
¾ yard

BACKING
5 yards - vertical seam(s)

OTHER SUPPLIES
7½ yards Medium Weight Fusible Interfacing

SAMPLE QUILT
Simply Happy by Dodi Poulson for Riley Blake Designs
(Outer Border), **Hopscotch - Rose Petals Nosegay** by
Jamie Fingal for RJR Fabrics

27

1 cut

From the white fabric, cut:

- (11) 3" strips across the width of the fabric – subcut 10 strips into 3" x 12½" rectangles. Each strip will yield 3 rectangles. Cut (1) 3" x 12½" rectangle from the remaining strip. You will have a **total of 31** rectangles.

- (7) 2½" strips across the width of the fabric. Set aside for the inner border.

From the print fabric, cut:

- (1) 3" strip across the width of the fabric – subcut the strip into (12) 3" squares.

- (3) 2½" strips across the width of the fabric – subcut each strip into 2½" squares. Each strip will yield 16 squares and a **total of 48** are needed.

2 prepare t-shirts

Wash and dry the shirts you have chosen. Trim off the neckband, the sleeves and the hem. Cut the front of the shirt away from the back, leaving as wide a margin as possible on either side of the portion of the shirt you would like to feature. Keep in mind that we will be trimming the featured portion to a 12½" square, so make sure it will fit in that measurement.

Cut (20) 13" squares of fusible interfacing. Center a square on top of the reverse side of the portion of each shirt you want to feature. Adhere the fusible to the reverse side of the shirt following the manufacturer's instructions. Once the fusible is bonded to the shirt, trim the featured portions to 12½" squares. Set aside for the moment.

3 make sashing rectangles

Pick up (14) 3" x 12½" white rectangles. Add a star point to 1 end of each strip by placing a 2½" print square on an angle (any angle) atop 1 end of the white rectangle with right sides facing. Make sure the print square is placed a little past

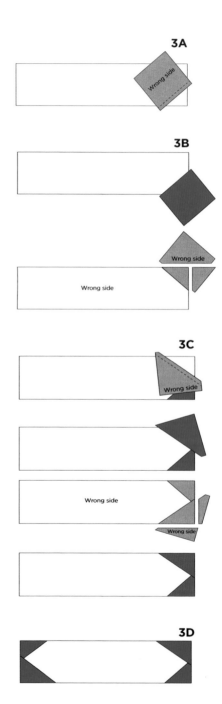

the halfway point. Sew ¼" in from the angled edge of the print square. Trim ¼" away from the sewn seam. **3A**

Press the piece flat, then turn the rectangle over and press the print square over the seam allowance. Trim the square so all edges are even with the rectangle. **3B**

Pick up the scrap you just trimmed away and place it on the other side of the rectangle with right sides facing. Make sure the edge of the scrap crosses over the first piece by at least ¼". Stitch ¼" in from the edge of the print. Trim the excess fabric away ¼" from the sewn seam. Make 14 sashing strips in this manner. **3C**

Repeat the instructions beginning on page 28 and add a star point to both ends of the 17 remaining white 3" x 12½" sashing rectangles. **3D**

4 make horizontal sashing strips

Sew a rectangle that has star points on 1 end to a 3" print square. Follow with a rectangle that has a star point on both ends. Add a print square, followed by a rectangle that has star points on both ends. Add another print square and end the row with a rectangle that has a star point on 1 end. Make 4 horizontal sashing strips in this manner. **4A**

5 arrange and sew

Lay out the T-shirt squares in rows. Each row is made up of **4 squares** across and **5 rows** are needed. Make sure any writing on the shirt squares is positioned so it can be read. Add a sashing rectangle that has 1 star leg between the squares in the first and last row. Notice that the star leg points in toward the center of the quilt and the writing on any square can be read. In rows 2, 3, and 4,

place a sashing strip that has star points on both ends between the T-shirt squares. Refer to the diagram on page 31, if necessary.

Sew the rows together, adding a horizontal sashing strip between each row to complete the center of the quilt. Refer to the diagram on page 31, if necessary.

6 inner border

Pick up the (7) 2½" strips that were set aside for the inner border. Sew the strips together end-to-end to make one long strip. Trim the borders from this strip.

Refer to Borders (pg. 118) in the Construction Basics to measure and cut the inner borders. The strips are approximately 70½" for the sides and approximately 60" for the top and bottom.

7 outer border

Cut (8) 5" strips across the width of the fabric. Sew the strips together end-to-end to make one long strip. Trim the borders from this strip.

t-shirt quilt

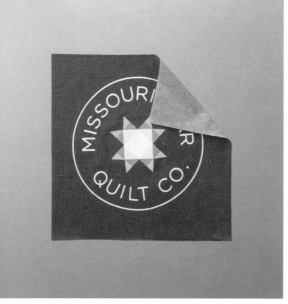

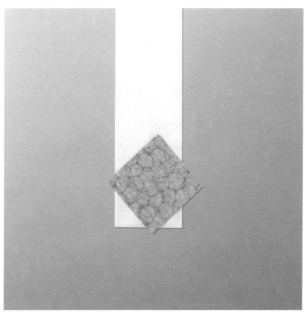

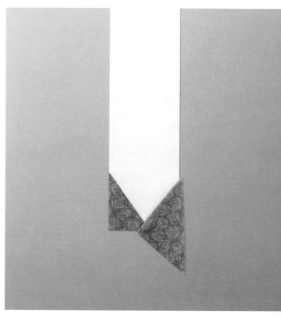

1 After washing, drying, and trimming a selected t-shirt, press a 13" square of fusible interfacing to the reverse side of the area of the t-shirt you want to feature. Trim to 12½".

2 Make sashing rectangles. Add a star point to 1 end of a strip by placing a 2½" print square on an angle atop 1 end of a white rectangle with right sides facing. Sew ¼" in from the angled edge of the square. Trim ¼" from the sewn seam.

3 Use the scrap you just trimmed to finish the star point on the opposite side of the rectangle.

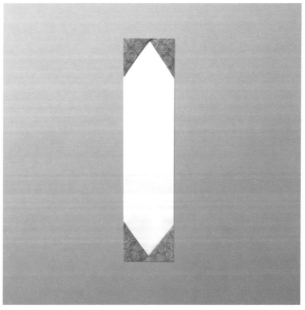

4 Trim the star point evenly with the end of the sashing rectangle. Make 14 sashing rectangles in this manner.

5 Repeat the instructions for making star points but add a star points to both ends of the 17 remaining white 3" x 12½" rectangles.

6 Add sashing rectangles and print squares between the t-shirt squares as needed. Refer to the diagram on page 31.

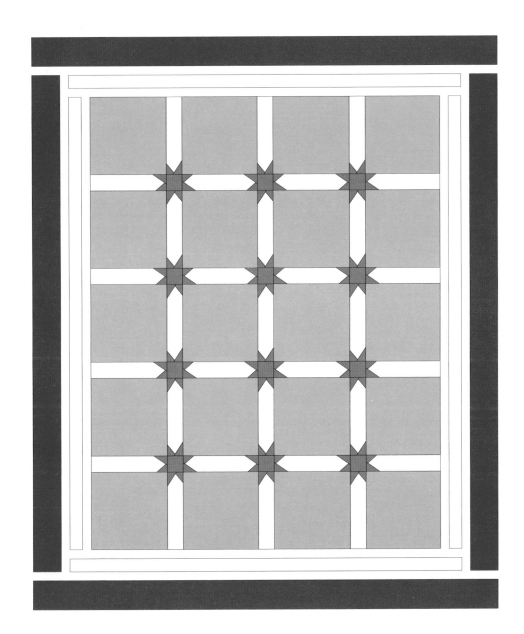

Refer to Borders (pg. 118) in the Construction Basics to measure and cut the outer borders. The strips are approximately 74½″ for the sides and approximately 69″ for the top and bottom.

8 quilt and bind

Layer the quilt with batting and backing and quilt. After the quilting is complete, square up the quilt and trim away all excess batting and backing. Add binding to complete the quilt. See Construction Basics (pg. 118) for binding instructions.

radiance

On warm evenings here in Hamilton, Missouri, you may notice a cute couple walking down a country lane, hand in hand. They're perfectly matched: snow white hair, glasses, and not quite five feet tall. For 40 years they've walked side by side, and their love story gets richer with every passing day.

Anita Scott was raised right here in town. Her parents owned a hardware store located in the very spot our Main Shop now stands. After high school, Anita ventured out and earned a college degree, but by age 27, she found herself back at home, keeping the books at the family shop and feeling quite certain she would never find love in this quiet little town.

Gary Henry was a teacher with big plans for the future. At 32 years old, he had earned three degrees in education, and was ready to climb the ladder from teacher to administrator. Eager for experience, he left his hometown of Quincy, Illinois, to accept a position at the elementary-middle school in Kingston, Missouri—less than 10 miles from Anita's Hamilton home.

One wintry day, Gary stopped in at Anita's hardware store to pick up something for school. Anita spotted him from the back room. Right off, she noticed how short he was. It wasn't often she met a man who could match her diminutive stature, and she was intrigued. She made her way to the front of the store where she quietly traded spots with the cashier.

Gary and Anita next bumped into one another at the bowling alley, and there was an instant connection.

Conversation was easy, and they found they had much in common: Old-fashioned values, a strong sense of family, and unwavering faith. From that moment on, the two were inseparable.

Anita's friends starting asking questions. Was Gary her boyfriend now? Were they in love? Is this IT? And so Anita asked Gary, "The girls keep asking. What should I say?"

"Well, you tell them we're going to get married."

And that was that. They were engaged! There was no ring, but that didn't matter. The date was set for summertime, but summer seemed so far away! Again and again they scooted that date up, finally settling on the last Saturday in March—just three short months after their very first meeting.

Pulling the wedding together was a bit of a whirlwind. With no time to order a gown, Anita traveled to the nearest boutique and bought a sample dress right off the rack, along with bridesmaids dresses and a suit for Gary.

On March 24, 1979, Gary and Anita were married in the United Methodist Church, right in Hamilton. This year they are celebrating 40 years of wedded bliss. Now in their golden years, Gary and Anita still love to spend time together, taking cross-country roadtrips and quiet strolls through town. Thank goodness Gary walked into Anita's hardware store so many years ago!

For the tutorial and everything you need to make this quilt visit:
www.msqc.co/celebrateblock19

33

materials

QUILT SIZE
70" x 70"

BLOCK SIZE
9½" finished

QUILT TOP
1 roll of 2½" print strips
1 package of 10" background squares

INNER BORDER
½ yard

BINDING
¾ yard

BACKING
4½ yards - vertical seam(s)

OTHER SUPPLIES
Missouri Star Quilt Co.-
    Burst Block Template

SAMPLE QUILT
Porcelain by 3 Sisters for Moda Fabrics

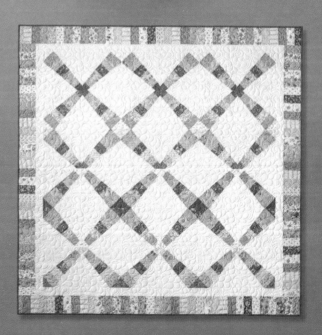

1 make strip sets

Select 7 strips from the roll. Use a dark fabric for the bottom strip and a light fabric at the top. Sew the strips together using a ¼" seam allowance. Press all seam allowances in the same direction. **Make 3. 1A**

2 cut

Trim the selvages from the strip set. Then align the 2 corners of the top of the template along the first seamline at the top of the strip set. (**Note:** placing a piece of clear tape from corner to corner can make alignment easier and keep the template placement consistent.) **2A**

Cut the shape, then turn the template 180˚, again aligning the 2 corners of the template with the first seamline of the strip set. Continue cutting across the strip set in this manner. Each strip set will yield 12 wedge-shaped pieces and a **total of 36** are needed. **2B**

3 block construction

Cut a 10" background square from corner to corner once on the diagonal. Fold each piece in half, matching up the 2 even edges. Finger press a crease in place along the fold line. **3A**

Fold the strip-pieced wedge in half. Finger press a crease on the fold. Align the fold on a background triangle with the fold on the strip-pieced wedge. Notice that the background triangle extends past the wedge on both ends. Pin in place, then stitch. Repeat for the other side. **3B 3C**

After both background triangles have been sewn in place, square up the block to 10" by aligning the ruler with the strip-pieced wedge and trimming all 4 sides of the block. **Make 36 blocks. 3D**

Block Size: 9½" finished

4 arrange and sew

Lay out the blocks in rows. Each row is made up of **6 blocks** and **6 rows** are needed. Refer to the diagram on page 39, if necessary. After the blocks have been sewn into rows, press the seam allowances of the odd rows toward the right and the even rows toward the left to make the seams nest.

Sew the rows together to complete the center of the quilt.

5 inner border

Cut (6) 2½" strips across the width of the fabric. Sew the strips together end-to-end to make one long strip. Trim the borders from this strip.

Refer to Borders (pg. 118) in the

2A

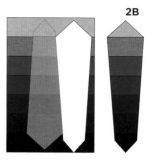

2B

1A

3A

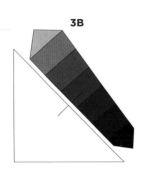

3B

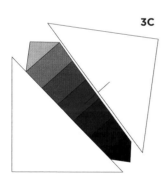

3C

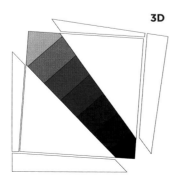

3D

Construction Basics to measure and cut the inner borders. The strips are approximately 57½" for the sides and approximately 61½" for the top and bottom.

6 outer border

Select 18 of the remaining strips from the roll. Sew 6 strips to make a strip set as before. Make 3 strip sets. Cut each set into 5" increments. Each set will yield (8) 5" x 12½" rectangles for a total of 24. There is a 2½" strip left. Cut (2) 2½" x 5" increments to use when making the side borders.

Measure the quilt top in several places vertically. (See Construction Basics on page 118 if necessary.) The top should measure approximately 61½" along the sides. Sew 5 strip-pieced rectangles together for each side to make a border that measures 60½" long unfinished. Add a single 2½" x 5" rectangle. Trim the border to fit your measurement. Make 2. Sew a border to either side of the quilt.

Measure the quilt in several places horizontally, being sure to include the borders you have just added. The border should measure approximately 70½". Sew 6 strip-pieced rectangles together and remove (1) 2½" strip so the border will be the correct size. Make 2 and sew 1 to the top of the quilt and 1 to the bottom.

Note: If you have a problem getting the pieced borders to fit exactly, adjust the length by using a scant ¼" seam allowance in several places if it is a little skimpy or use a bit larger seam allowance in several places if it's a bit too long.

7 quilt and bind

Layer the quilt with batting and backing and quilt. After the quilting is complete, square up the quilt and trim away all excess batting and backing. Add binding to complete the quilt. See Construction Basics (pg. 118) for binding instructions.

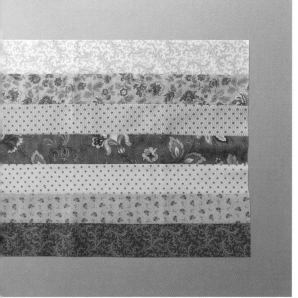

1 Select 7 strips from the roll. Use a dark fabric for the bottom strip and a light fabric at the top. Sew the strips together using a ¼" seam allowance. Press all seam allowances in the same direction.

2 Align the two corners of the top of the template along the first seamline at the top of the strip set. Cut the shape, then turn the template 180 degrees. Continue cutting across the strip set in this manner.

3 Cut a 10" background square from corner to corner once on the diagonal. Fold each piece in half, matching up the 2 even edges and finger press a crease in place along the fold.

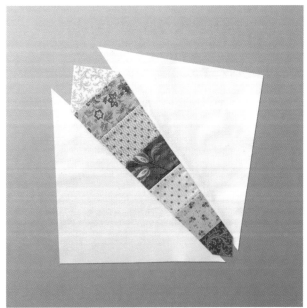

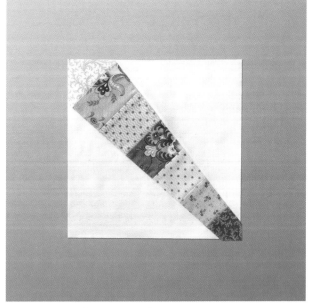

4 Fold the strip-pieced wedge in half and finger press the fold. Align the fold of the wedge with the fold of the background fabric. Stitch a background triangle to both sides of the wedge.

5 Square up the block by trimming the background triangles evenly with the corners of the strip-pieced wedge.

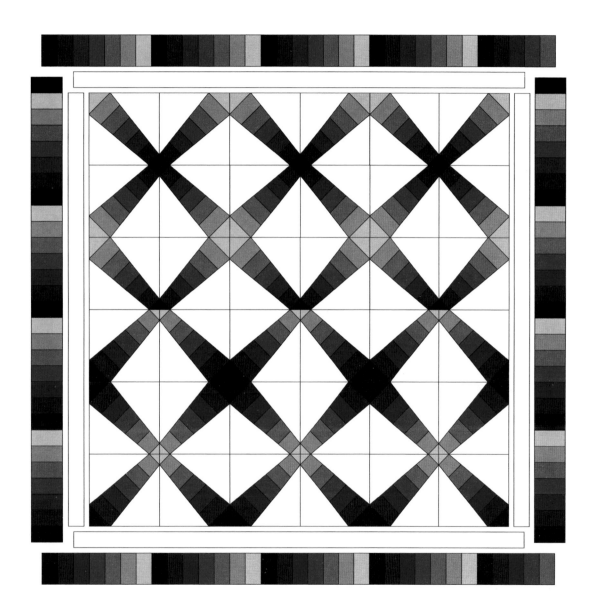

crown jewel

Sending children off to school can be tough. I know, I've sent off far too many myself! Before they leave, I always make sure they have a little piece of home to take with them in the form of a handmade quilt. No matter where you may go, quilts make you feel right at home.

When Carrie graduated from high school, friends and family congratulated her with thoughtful little gifts and greeting cards stuffed with 20 dollar bills, but nothing touched her young heart quite like the quilt that had been handstitched by her very own grandmother.

Grandma had a tradition of giving quilts to mark special occasions. From the very first baby quilt up to elegantly pieced wedding gifts, everyone in the family looked forward to Grandma's quilts.

Carrie's graduation quilt was made up of flower basket blocks in rose, navy, and cream calicos. The piecing was done on Grandma's black antique Singer, but each quilting stitch was the work of her own two hands. Carrie had watched Grandma quilt so many times, she could close her eyes and picture the shape of Grandma's agile hands as she guided the needle up and down through the layers of fabric and batting.

When Carrie went off to college, the graduation quilt went with her. It added a cozy touch to her tiny, bare dorm room, and whenever she felt a bit homesick or overwhelmed, she snuggled up under that quilt and felt the stress melt away.

That quilt followed her back home after college graduation, and then to her first home with her handsome young husband. It was still on Carrie's bed when she brought her first son home from the hospital, just weeks before Grandma passed away.

Over the years, that quilt had been through the wash more times than Carrie could count. It had hung on the clothesline as the breeze blew the fresh scent of summer through its fibers. It had been loved and used until the binding was threadbare and the batting started to escape along the edges.

On Carrie's 30th birthday, a sweet aunt surprised her with a beautiful new quilt. It was pink and blue, the same colors as Grandma's quilt, but bright and fresh, with no rips or tears. Carrie spread the new quilt over her bed, but couldn't bear to part with the graduation quilt. And so it stayed, worn and comfy and full of memories, layered underneath the pretty new quilt.

This summer marks the 20th anniversary of Carrie's high school graduation, ten of those years without Grandma. Time has flown at the speed of light, it seems, but that quilt remains, and perhaps always will. Because even now, when she climbs into bed, she feels that safe, comfortable feeling that only comes from a quilt made with love.

For the tutorial and everything you need to make this quilt visit:

www.msqc.co/celebrateblock19

41

materials

QUILT SIZE
77" x 77"

BLOCK SIZE
16" finished

QUILT TOP
3½ yards black fabric - includes outer border
2¾ yards of background fabric - includes
    inner border
1¼ yards of gold or complementary fabric
    of your choice

BINDING
¾ yard

BACKING
5 yards - vertical seam(s) or 2½ yards of 108" wide

SAMPLE QUILT
Bella Solids Golden Wheat and Bella Solids Black
by Moda Fabrics

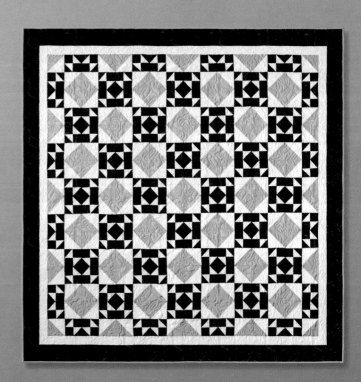

1 cut

From the black fabric, cut:

- (32) 2½" strips across the width of the fabric - subcut each strip into 2½" squares. Each strip will yield 16 squares and a **total of 512** are needed.

- (8) 5" strips across the width of the fabric - set aside for the outer border.

From the background fabric, cut:

- (4) 10" strips across the width of the fabric – subcut each strip into 10" squares. Each strip will yield 4 squares and a **total of 16** squares are needed.

- (23) 2½" strips across the width of the fabric – subcut each of 16 strips into 2½" squares. Each strip will yield 16 squares and a **total of 256** are needed. Set aside the remaining 7 strips for the inner border.

From the gold fabric, cut:

- (4) 10" strips across the width of the fabric – subcut each strip into 10" squares. Each strip will yield 4 squares and a **total of 16** squares are needed.

2 make large half-square triangles

On the reverse side of each of the 10" background squares, draw a line from corner to corner twice on the diagonal. Layer a marked 10" background square with a 10" gold square with right sides facing. Sew on both sides of each of the drawn lines using a ¼" seam allowance. Cut the sewn squares in half horizontally and vertically. Then cut on the drawn lines. Each set of sewn squares will yield 8 half-square triangle units and a **total of 128** are needed. Open and press the seam allowance toward the dark fabric. Square up each half-square triangle to 4½". **2A**

3 block construction

Pick up 16 black 2½" squares and 16 background 2½" squares. Mark a line from corner to corner once on the diagonal on the reverse side of each background square. Layer a marked background square with a 2½" black

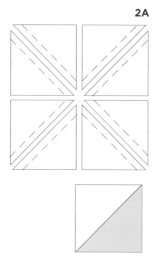

2A

square. Sew on the drawn line. Cut the excess fabric away ¼" from the sewn seam. Open to reveal a half-square triangle unit and press the seam allowance toward the dark fabric. Make 16. **3A**

Pick up (16) 2½" black squares and 16 half-square triangle units. Sew a square to a half-square triangle. Make (8) 4-patch units. Sew 2 together as shown. For the sake of clarity, we will call them "paired 4-patches." **3B**

Sew a large half-square triangle unit to both ends of a paired 4-patch unit as shown. Make 2 rows like this. **3C**

Sew 4 large half-square triangles together in a 4-patch formation to make the center section of the row.

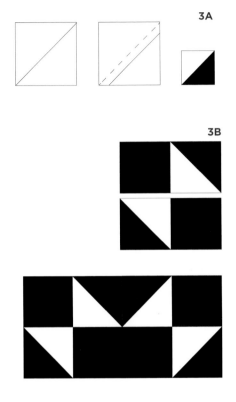

3A

3B

3C

3D

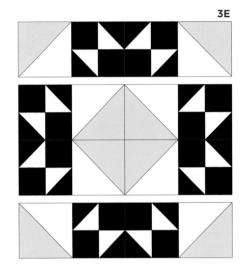

3E

Add a paired 4-patch unit to both sides of the center section to complete the row. **3D**

Sew the 3 rows together to complete 1 block. **Make 16. 3E**

Block Size: 16″ finished

4 arrange and sew

Lay out the blocks in rows. Each row is made up of **4 blocks** and **4 rows** are needed. After the blocks have been sewn into rows, press the seam allowances of the odd-numbered rows toward the right and the even-numbered rows toward the left to make the seams nest. Sew the rows together to complete the center of the quilt.

5 inner border

Pick up the (7) 2½″ strips that were set aside. Sew the strips together end-to-end to make one long strip. Trim the borders from this strip.

Refer to Borders (pg. 118) in the Construction Basics to measure and cut the inner borders. The strips are approximately 64½″ for the sides and approximately 68½″ for the top and bottom.

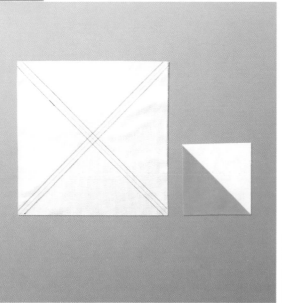

1 On the reverse side of a 10" background square, draw a line from corner to corner twice on the diagonal. Sew on both sides of the drawn lines using a ¼" seam allowance. Cut the sewn squares in half vertically and horizontally, then cut on the drawn lines. Open to reveal 8 half-square triangle units. Square each to 4½".

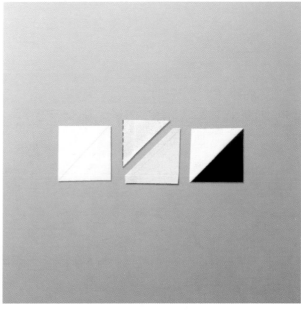

2 Draw a line once on the diagonal on the reverse side of each 2½" background square. Layer a marked square with a black square and sew on the marked line. Trim ¼" from the sewn seam. Open to reveal 1 half-square triangle unit.

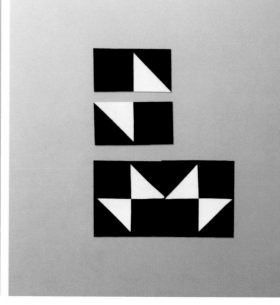

3 Pick up (16) 2½" black squares and 16 half-square triangle units. Sew them into 4-patch units as shown. Sew (2) 4-patch units together to make "paired 4-patches."

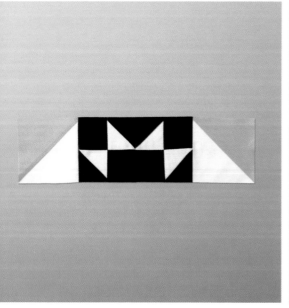

4 Sew a large half-square triangle unit to both ends of a paired 4-patch unit to make the top and bottom rows of the block.

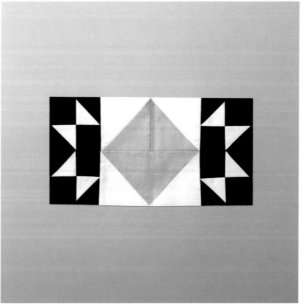

5 Sew 4 large half-square triangle units together to make the center section of the middle row. Sew a paired 4-patch unit to both sides of the center section to complete the row.

6 Sew the 3 rows together to complete the block.

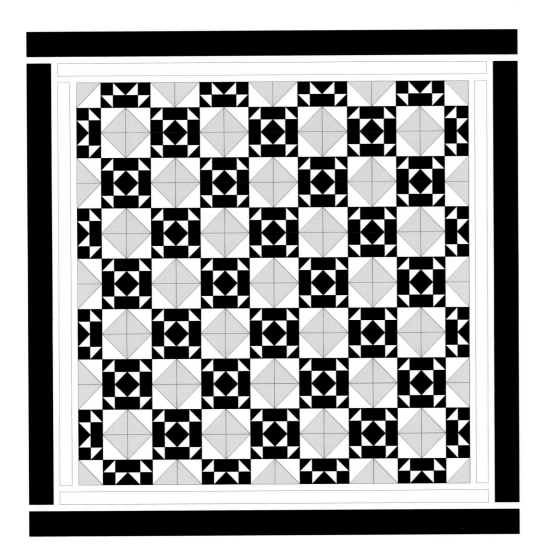

6 outer border

Pick up the 5″ strips you cut and set aside earlier. Sew the strips together end-to-end to make one long strip. Trim the borders from this strip.

Refer to Borders (pg. 118) in the Construction Basics to measure and cut the outer borders. The strips are approximately 68½″ for the sides and approximately 77½″ for the top and bottom.

7 quilt and bind

Layer the quilt with batting and backing and quilt. After the quilting is complete, square up the quilt and trim away all excess batting and backing. Add binding to complete the quilt. See Construction Basics (pg. 118) for binding instructions.

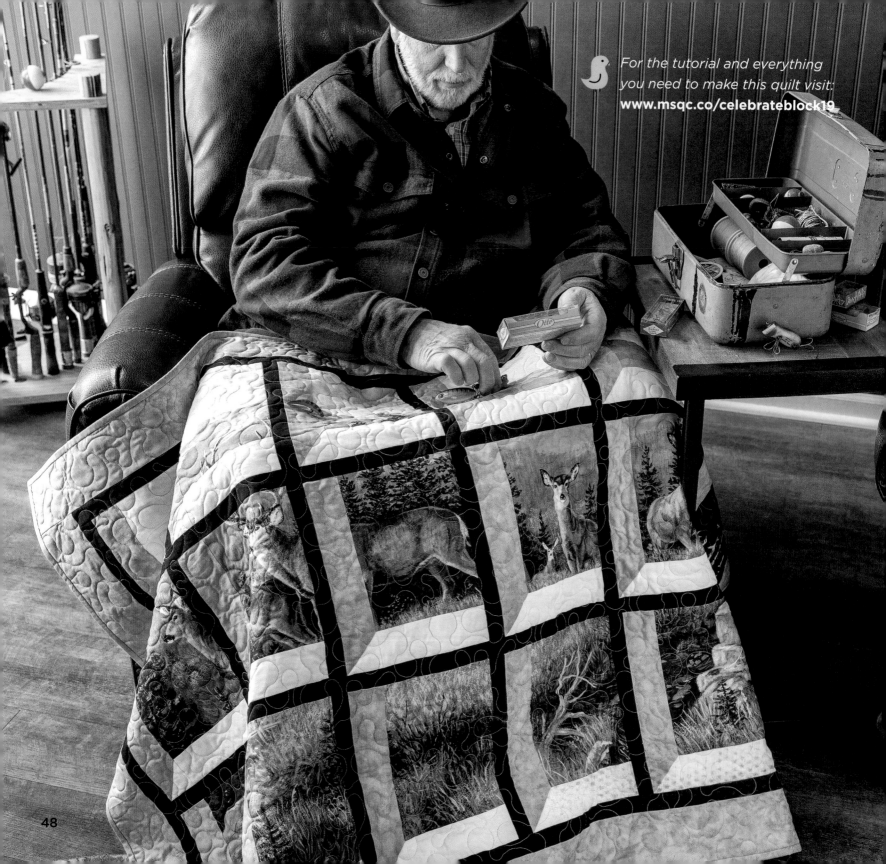

48

attic window panel

Jenny and her husband Ron have seven children, each as unique and fun as can be. And each carries within them a little piece of their parents. Some similarities are noticeable right away like hair color or a sprinkling of freckles, but even more special are the talents and personality traits that reflect the influence of their good parents.

Hillary, for example, has a kind soul, just like her dad. But her passion for music came straight from Jenny. What a lovely combo!

Sarah is a bit of a thrill-seeker. She inherited Ron's love of motorcycles and cars. She loves to ride fast and feel the wind blow through her hair. And, like her mom, she has a quick wit and loves to laugh.

Natalie is the one who got her looks from her mother. One glance and you'll recognize that friendly smile. And not only do they look alike, they sew alike, too. In fact, Natalie is such a talented quilter, she was selected to host our *Create Better Bindings* video course, and she absolutely rocked it!

Jake is great at building with his hands, a talent he inherited from Ron. But you'd better be careful 'round April Fool's, because he's a fantastic prankster—just like his mom! (Bet you didn't know that about our sweet Jenny!)

Josh takes after Ron with his gentle, nurturing ways and his analytical brain. And Al is always the life of the party, just like his spotlight-loving momma.

One trait that is common among all the Doan siblings is a serious dose of creativity. These kids are makers, and it's no wonder! Creativity is one trait that was passed down from both Jenny and Ron. When asked about that innovative, can-do attitude, Al shared this fun story:

"One of my favorite memories is making a 'space derby' glider with Dad. Just like its better-known cousin, the pinewood derby car, a space derby gilder starts out as a simple block of wood. Each Cub Scout gets to carve and decorate their block of wood, add fins and a rubber band-powered propeller, and race it along strings with the other boys.

I knew most of the boys in my troop would be making ships that basically looked like ... a block of wood, but I wanted mine to look like a spaceship. So Dad and I sat and looked at that block of wood as we tried to figure a way to make my vision a reality. Finally, Dad grabbed his tools and we went to work.

He strapped the wooden block to a big drill bit and handed me a sander. Then he turned on the drill and I started sanding. It was our own makeshift lathe. After a few minutes, we had a perfectly shaped rocket ship. Honestly, it was pretty dang impressive. But that's Dad. He can do anything. He just figures out a way. And as we grew up, we loved doing the same."

materials

QUILT SIZE
65" x 43¼"

BLOCK SIZE
9½" x 10¾" finished

QUILT TOP
(1) 42" x 28" panel
½ yard white fabric
1¼ yards tan fabric – includes outer border
¾ yard black fabric – includes inner border

BINDING
½ yard

BACKING
3 yards - vertical seam(s)

SAMPLE QUILT
High Ridge Crossing by Terry Doughty
for Northcott Fabrics

1 cut

Remove the selvages and trim the panel to 42" x 27¾". Subcut (3) 9¼" strips across the width of the trimmed panel. Subcut (6) 7" x 9¼" rectangles from each strip for a **total of 18** rectangles. Keep them organized by stacking them in 3 piles of the 6 rectangles cut from each strip.

From the white fabric, cut (5) 2½" strips across the width of the fabric. Subcut 2½" x 7" rectangles from 4 of the strips. Each strip will yield 5 rectangles and a **total of 18** are needed. From the remainder of the cut strip and 1 additional 2½" strip, subcut 2½" squares. One full strip will yield 16 squares and a **total of 18** are needed.

From the tan fabric, cut (6) 2½" strips across the width of the fabric. Subcut 2½" x 11¼" rectangles from the strips. Each strip will yield 3 rectangles and a **total of 18** are needed. Set the remainder of the fabric aside for the outer border.

From the black fabric, cut (13) 1½" strips across the width of the

fabric. Subcut 6 strips into 1½" x 11¼" rectangles. Each strip will yield 3 rectangles and a **total of 18** are needed for the vertical sashing. Sew 3 strips together end-to-end to make one long strip. Subcut the long strip into (2) 1½" x 57½" horizontal sashing rectangles. Set the remaining 4 strips aside for the inner border.

2 sew

Sew a 2½" x 7" white rectangle to the bottom of each rectangle cut from the panel. Take care to keep these units in the same order as before. Make 18. **2A**

On the reverse side of a 2½" white square, mark a line from corner to corner once on the diagonal either by folding the square and pressing in a crease or by marking it with a pencil. **2B**

Snowball a 2½" x 11¼" tan rectangle by placing a marked square atop 1 end. Sew on the marked line, making note of its orientation in the diagram. Trim the excess fabric away ¼" from the sewn seam. Make 18. **2C**

2A

2B

2C

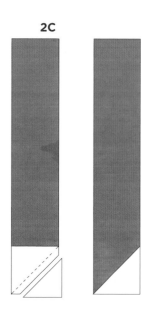

Sew a snowballed rectangle to the left side of a panel unit. **2D**

Sew a vertical sashing rectangle to the right side of the panel unit to complete the block. **2E**

Make 18 blocks.

Block Size: 9½" x 10¾" finished

3 arrange and sew

Lay out the blocks in rows paying particular attention to the order of the blocks. Refer to the diagram on page 55, if necessary. Each row is made up of **6 blocks** and **3 rows** are needed. Sew the blocks together in rows.

Sew the rows together, separating each row with a horizontal sashing rectangle to complete the quilt center.

4 inner border

Pick up the 1½" strips for the inner border and sew them together end-to-end to make one long strip. Trim the borders from this strip. Notice there is not an inner border on the right side of the quilt center.

Refer to Borders (pg. 118) in the Construction Basics to measure and cut the inner borders. The strip for the side is approximately 34¾" long and the strips for the top and bottom are approximately 58½" long.

5 outer border

Cut (6) 4" strips across the width of the fabric. Sew the strips together end-to-end to make one long strip. Trim the borders from this strip.

Refer to Borders (pg. 118) in the Construction Basics to measure and cut the outer borders. The strips are approximately 36¾" for the sides and approximately 65½" for the top and bottom.

6 quilt and bind

Layer the quilt with batting and backing and quilt. After the quilting is complete, square up the quilt and trim away all excess batting and backing. Add binding to complete the quilt. See Construction Basics (pg. 118) for binding instructions.

2D

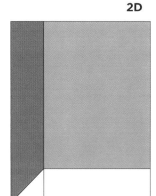

2E

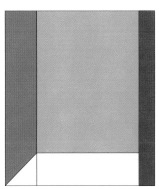

1 Sew a 2½" x 7" white rectangle to the bottom of each rectangle cut from the panel.

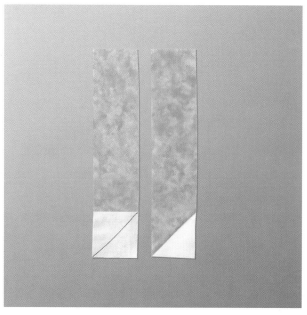

2 Snowball a 2½" x 11¼" tan rectangle by placing a marked 2½" square atop one end. Sew on the marked line. Trim the excess fabric away ¼" from the sewn seam. Notice the orientation of the marked angle.

3 Sew a snowballed rectangle to the left side of the panel unit.

4 Add a vertical sashing rectangle to the right side of the panel unit to complete the block.

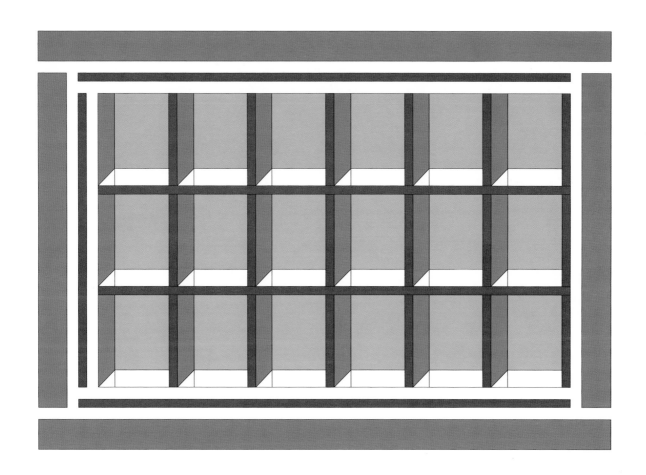

For the tutorial and everything
you need to make this quilt visit:
www.msqc.co/celebrateblock19

disappearing double pinwheel

I love the idea of high school sweethearts. Ron and I weren't dating way back then, but these stories just melt my heart! David, a friend of mine, told me the story of his best friends' wedding and how it all began with a simple handful of candy.

When my friends, John and McCall, announced they were getting married, my reaction was, "Finally!" By the time John proposed, they had been dating for almost a decade and McCall was wondering if he would ever get around to it! But they were definitely meant to be, from their very first meeting in the high school cafeteria all the way down the aisle of their church almost a decade later.

Back in the day, when we would sit together in our college dorms and complain about being single, John would always just smirk and say, "It's not that hard! Just use 'the move.'" We rolled our eyes at that one because when we were in high school, John's signature move wasn't too slick. Being a teenager, it was hard for him to talk to his crush, McCall. So, how did he do it? He threw jawbreaker candies at her over the lunch table to get her attention! To this day, John insists that throwing candy at a girl you like is "the move."

Needless to say, "the move" did work for John and their long-awaited wedding day finally happened. John cleaned up nicely and McCall was stunning in her mother's wedding dress. His father, a minister, gave them their vows, and cheers erupted from the guests when they were pronounced man and wife. Toasts were made to the happy couple and the revelry was well underway when our friend Richard suddenly disappeared! Richard was always a prankster and we got a bit worried as the time came for our group dance. What was he up to?

Just as John and McCall walked out to the dance floor, Richard snuck in through a side entrance and pressed something into my hand. "When the dance is done, you know what to do," he whispered with a mischievous grin. When I opened my hand, I found jawbreakers! Richard had traveled all the way back to our hometown, found the same brand of candy that John used, and made it back just in time.

Once the group dance had ended, Richard gave the signal and the air was filled with jawbreakers raining down on the happy couple. They looked surprised and then doubled over with laughter when they realized what it was. The newlyweds walked right over to Richard and gave him a tight hug. Of course, the very next thing they did was hand him a broom to clean up all the candy!

A couple of years have passed since then, and John and McCall are still the wonderful couple we knew before their wedding. They keep a jar of those jawbreakers on the hearth next to their wedding photo as a reminder of how it all began. It just goes to show that growing older doesn't necessarily mean growing up.

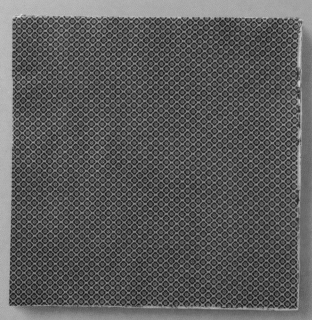

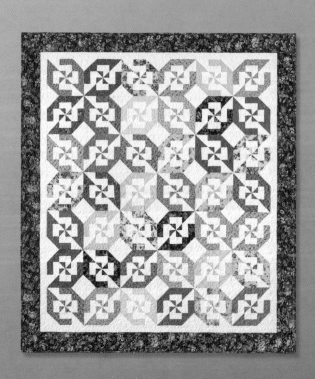

materials

QUILT SIZE
81" x 92"

BLOCK SIZE
11" finished

QUILT TOP
1 package of 10" print squares
1 package of 10" background squares

INNER BORDER
¾ yard

OUTER BORDER
1¾ yards

BINDING
¾ yard

BACKING
8½ yards - vertical seam(s) or 2¾ yards 108" wide

SAMPLE QUILT
Bed of Roses by Edyta Sitar for Andover Fabrics

1 make half-square triangles

Layer a 10" print square with a 10" background square with right sides facing. Sew all the way around the outside edge using a ¼" seam allowance. Cut the sewn squares from corner to corner twice on the diagonal. Each pair of sewn squares will yield 4 half-square triangle units and a **total of 168** are needed. Square each unit to 6½" and press the seam allowance toward the darker fabric. Keep all matching units together. **1A**

Sew 4 half-square triangles together in a 4-patch formation to make a pinwheel. Press the seam allowances in the top row toward the right and the bottom row toward the left. **1B**

Measure the sewn block. Divide the measurement by 3 so you can cut the block into thirds. It should be about 4¼". Divide that number in half if you would like to use the center seam as a guide. If you're using the center seam, measure out 2⅛" inches (or half of

your measurement) and cut on either side of the center seam horizontally and vertically. **1C**

2 turn and sew

The center pinwheel does not move. Turn each of the center pieces on the outer edge, the upper left corner, and the lower right corner 90° clockwise and the remaining 2 corner pieces 180°. Refer to the diagram for placement purposes if necessary. **2A**

Sew the pieces into rows as shown, then sew the rows together to complete the block. **Make 42** blocks. **2B**

Block Size: 11" finished

3 arrange in rows

Arrange the blocks into rows. Each row is made up of **6 blocks** across and **7 rows** are needed. Follow the diagram on page 63 and lay out the blocks. Notice how every other block is turned. When you are happy with the way the quilt is laid out, sew the blocks together. Press

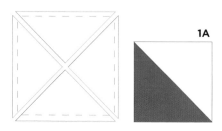

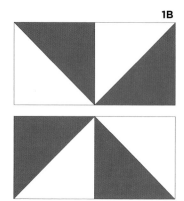

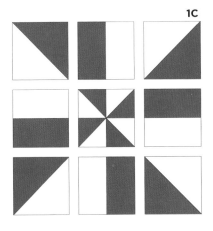

1C

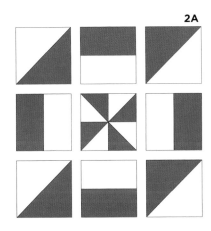

2A

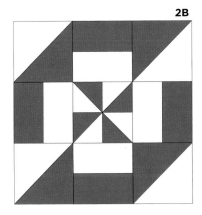

2B

the odd rows toward the left and the even rows toward the right to make the seams nest.

Sew the rows together.

4 inner border

Cut (8) 2½" strips across the width of the fabric. Sew the strips together end-to-end to make one long strip. Trim the borders from this strip.

Refer to Borders (pg. 118) in the Construction Basics to measure and cut the inner borders. The strips are approximately 77½" for the sides and approximately 70½" for the top and bottom.

5 outer border

Cut (9) 6" strips across the width of the fabric. Sew the strips together end-to-end to make one long strip. Trim the borders from this strip.

Refer to Borders (pg. 118) in the Construction Basics to measure and cut the outer borders. The strips are approximately 81½" for the sides and approximately 81½" for the top and bottom.

6 quilt and bind

Layer the quilt with batting and backing and quilt. After the quilting is complete, square up the quilt and trim away all excess batting and backing. Add binding to complete the quilt. See Construction Basics (pg. 118) for binding instructions.

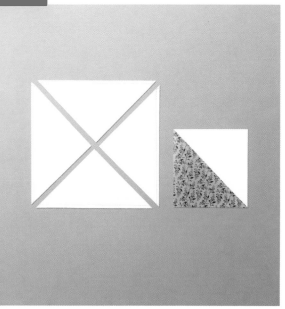

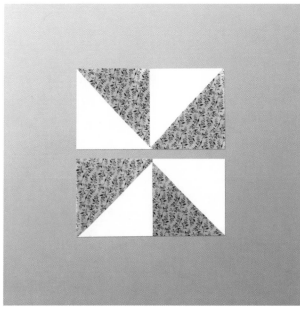

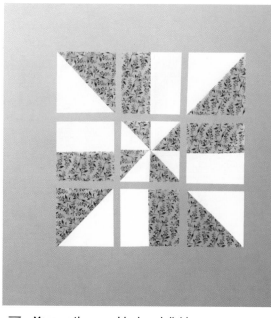

1 Layer a 10" print square with a 10" background square with right sides facing. Sew all the way around the outer edge using a ¼" seam allowance. Cut the sewn squares from corner to corner twice on the diagonal. Open to reveal 4 half-square triangle units. Square each to 6½".

2 Sew 4 half-square triangles together into a 4-patch to make a pinwheel.

3 Measure the sewn block and divide the measurement by 3. It should be about 4¼". Divide that number in half if you would like to use the center seam line as a cutting guide. Cut on either side of the center seam line horizontally and vertically.

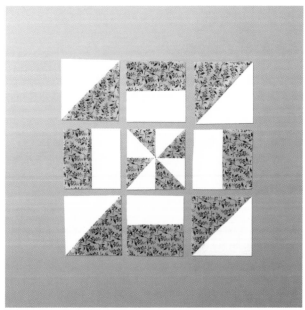

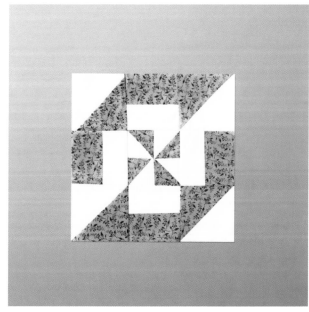

4 Turn each of the center pieces on the outer edge, the upper left corner, and the lower right corner 90° clockwise and the remaining 2 corner pieces 180° The center pinwheel does not move.

5 Sew the rearranged pieces back together as shown to complete the block.

For the tutorial and everything
you need to make this quilt visit:
www.msqc.co/celebrateblock19

periwinkle
on point

Teachers have a big job on their hands. With more than 3.1 million teachers in the U.S., they're one of the largest professions, but one of the most underappreciated. Did you know most teachers work about 50 hours a week? That adds up to a whopping 400 hours of overtime each year per teacher. Many teachers have second jobs too. Over 30% seek out additional employment to help make ends meet. Teaching is a challenge, but one that is met with heart. These wonderful, dedicated individuals care so deeply that they are willing to overcome tough obstacles. It's said, "It takes a big heart to shape little minds," and I truly believe it.

For example, 90% of teachers purchase supplies for students who can't afford them. Per teacher, that's an average of $500 a year. During the cold months, one out of three teachers buys coats, mittens, and other clothing to keep their students warm. It's obvious that teaching goes beyond the classroom. Students have many needs and approaching academics without noticing that a student is hungry, tired, cold, or dirty is impossible. As the old saying goes, "Students don't care how much you know until they know how much you care." Teachers reach out, they care, and then they challenge you to learn something new! The percentage of people who believe a teacher can change the course of a student's life is 98%. Teachers can make a difference!

Take a moment to think back on the teachers who have shaped your life. What could you do to show a teacher you care? One of my friends wrote a letter to her middle school English teacher, expressing her thanks for what she learned in his class.

His response reflects the feelings many teachers have when they see the progress their students make. Teaching isn't always easy on a day-by-day basis while experiencing the struggle of trying to help students make connections, but it's often rewarding to see who students become.

Nichole,

It's so good to hear from you! I have to say that the picture I have of you in my mind's eye probably resembles you only slightly now. One of the wonders of growing old(er!). Thank you for the kind words. I truly love my job, and it becomes an enormous blessing when I hear I've done good in the world. Thank you for the smile you have brought to me today. It reflects a true, deep warming of my heart.

Mr. Adams

The first week of May is Teacher Appreciation Week, but you don't have to wait for it to say thank you! Reach out now and remember them, because chances are, they remember you! One famous teacher, Taylor Mali, put it well, "Here, let me break it down for you, so you know what I say is true: Teachers? Teachers make a difference! Now what about you?"

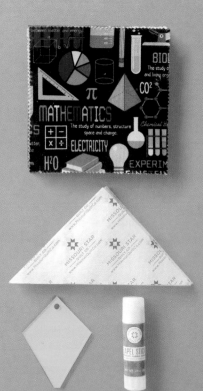

materials

QUILT SIZE
71" x 71"

BLOCK SIZE
7" finished

QUILT TOP
4 packages of 5" print squares
3¾ yards of background fabric - includes inner border

OUTER BORDER
1¼ yards

BINDING
¾ yard

BACKING
4½ yards - vertical seam(s)

OTHER SUPPLIES
Lapel Stick (glue stick)
2 packages Mini Wacky Web Triangle Papers
Missouri Star Quilt Co. - Mini Periwinkle
    (Wacky Web) Template

SAMPLE QUILT
Big Bang by Deborah Edwards for Northcott

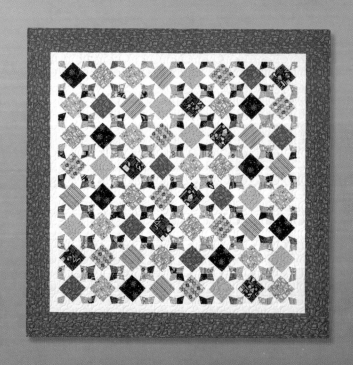

1 cut

From the background fabric, cut:

- (53) 2½" strips across the width of the fabric – subcut 47 strips into 2½" x 3½" rectangles. Each strip will yield 11 rectangles and a **total of 512** are needed. Set the remaining 6 strips aside for the inner border.

From the 5" print squares, select 128 medium to dark assorted squares. Set all remaining pieces aside for another project. Choose 64 squares for the centers of the blocks. From each of

the remaining squares, cut 4 periwinkle shapes using the Mini template.

Note: by folding each 5" square in half vertically and horizontally, 4 periwinkle shapes can be cut at once. Keep all matching pieces together. You will have a **total of 256** periwinkle shapes.

2 block construction

Pick up 4 matching periwinkle shapes, (8) 2½" x 3½" background rectangles, (1) 5" square and 4 Wacky Web papers.

Using the Lapel Stick, run a line of glue onto a paper from the corner to the center of the long edge of the paper. **2A**

Place a periwinkle shape onto the paper atop the glue with the right side facing up. Place a 2½" x 3½" rectangle atop the periwinkle shape with right sides together. Stitch in place using a ¼" seam allowance. Press the rectangle over the seam allowance. Repeat for the other side of the periwinkle shape. **2B 2C 2D 2E**

2A

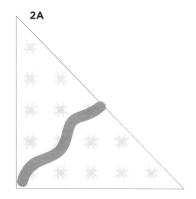

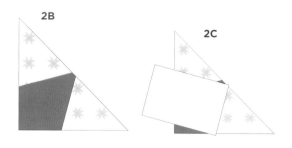

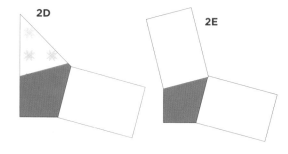

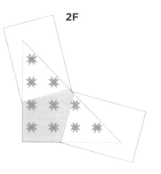

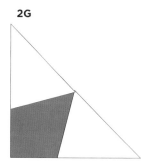

Turn the paper over so the fabric is facing down. Use the paper as a pattern and trim all excess fabric away. Make 4 periwinkle units and remove the paper. **2F 2G**

Fold a 5″ square in half vertically and horizontally and finger press the crease in place along each edge. Fold the periwinkle units in half and finger press a crease in place. Align the crease in the periwinkle unit to the crease in the 5″ square and pin in place with right sides facing. Sew a periwinkle unit to opposite sides of the 5″ square. Press the seam allowances toward the center square. **2H**

Add a periwinkle unit to the 2 remaining sides of the square and press the seams toward the center. **Make 64** blocks. **2I 2J**

Block Size: 7″ finished

3 arrange and sew

Lay out the blocks in rows. Each row is made up of **8 blocks** and **8 rows** are needed. After the blocks have been sewn into rows, press the seam allowances of the odd-numbered rows toward the right and the even-numbered rows toward the left to make the seams nest.

Sew the rows together to complete the center of the quilt.

4 inner border

Pick up the (6) 2½″ strips that were set aside. Sew the strips together end-to-end to make one long strip. Trim the borders from this strip.

Refer to Borders (pg. 118) in the Construction Basics to measure and cut the inner borders. The strips are approximately 56½″ for the sides and approximately 60½″ for the top and bottom.

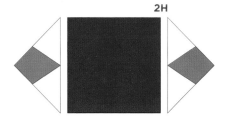

2H

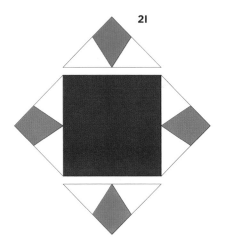

2I

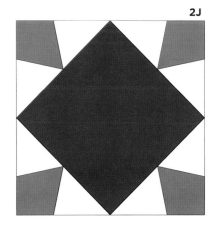

2J

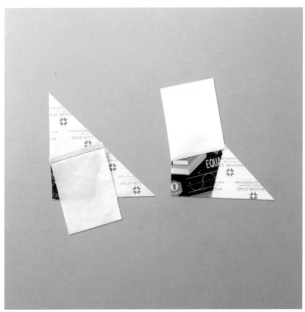

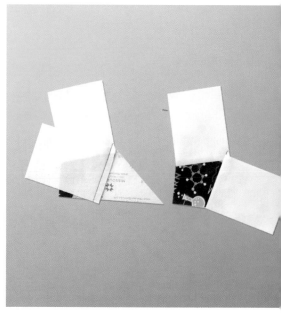

1 Using the Lapel Stick, run a line of glue onto a paper from the corner to the center of the long edge of the paper. Place a periwinkle shape (right side facing up) atop the line of glue.

2 Place a 2½" x 3½" background rectangle atop the periwinkle shape with right sides facing. Stitch in place. Press the rectangle over the seam allowance.

3 Add a background rectangle to the other side of the periwinkle shape with right sides facing. Sew in place and press the rectangle over the seam allowance.

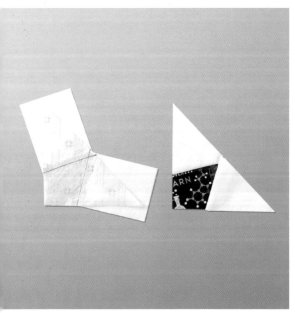

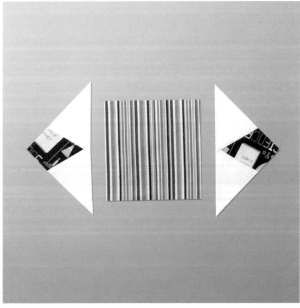

4 Turn the paper over so the fabric is facing down. Use the edge of the paper as a pattern and trim all excess fabric away. Make 4 periwinkle units and remove the paper.

5 Sew a periwinkle unit to opposite sides of a 5" print square. Press the seam allowances toward the square.

6 Sew a periwinkle unit to opposite sides of a 5" print square. Press the seam allowances toward the square.

5 outer border

Cut (7) 6" strips across the width of the fabric. Sew the strips together end-to-end to make one long strip. Trim the borders from this strip.

Refer to Borders (pg. 118) in the Construction Basics to measure and cut the outer borders. The strips are approximately 60½" for the sides and approximately 71½" for the top and bottom.

6 quilt and bind

Layer the quilt with batting and backing and quilt. After the quilting is complete, square up the quilt and trim away all excess batting and backing. Add binding to complete the quilt. See Construction Basics (pg. 118) for binding instructions.

denim snowball quilt

As teenagers, we were sure we had it all figured out … until we left home! I saw a sign that gave me a good laugh: "Teenagers! Tired of being harassed by your parents? Act now! Move out, get a job, and pay your bills, while you still know everything!" Young people are so capable and so sure of themselves, and that's not a bad thing. But there was definitely a time in my life when I realized that my parents actually knew what they were talking about!

Do you remember the advice your parents used to give you? A few phrases stand out and I realized that I now say them to my own children. In the middle of cleaning they probably heard something like, "If you've got time to lean, you've got time to clean." As they walked out the door to school I called after them, "Remember who you are!" When faced with comparison I would say, "Do a thing as best as you can and rejoice with him who can do it better." And if they were seeking advice with a tough situation, I often told them, "It's nice to be important, but it's more important to be nice."

I asked around and my friends shared some of the sage wisdom they'd heard from their own parents:

Jenna said, "'Fair is a place you go for a ride.' At first, I didn't understand why my mom said it, but now I see that she was trying to teach us to be grateful for what we had."

Trisa said, "My dad's reply to fixing anything was always 'K.I.S.S.—Keep it simple stupid.' It was his way of telling us not to complicate things."

Janet said, "'Garbage in, Garbage out.' Be aware of what you choose to let into your mind and heart, it shapes everything in your world."

Brent said, "Nothing good happens after midnight!"

Denise said, "If someone makes you mad, kill them with kindness."

Glenette said, "Take care of the little things, then you won't have big things to worry about!"

Meg said, "Remember who you are and what you stand for!"

Susan said, "Never tell anyone how good you are at something, if you are really good they will tell you."

Ceshia said, "My mom always told me to be who I wanted to be, not what others expected of me."

Crissa said, "Always tell the truth, then you'll always remember what you said!"

Becky said, "You are who you hang out with. I still find myself thinking about that daily. Be friends with the best and you will follow suit."

I am so grateful to have been raised by kind, wise parents. As we embark on our own journeys in this world, we carry their wisdom along with us. It really does help us remember who we are and where we came from.

For the tutorial and everything you need to make this quilt visit:
www.msqc.co/celebrateblock19

materials

QUILT SIZE
68" x 77½"

BLOCK SIZE
9½" finished

QUILT TOP*
1¼ yards light blue denim
1¾ yards dark blue denim
1 yard black denim**

BORDER
1 yard**

BINDING
½ yard

BACKING
4¾ yards - vertical seam(s)

SAMPLE QUILT
Indigo Denim by Robert Kaufman Fabrics

*NOTE: The yardage for this quilt is based on 56" useable fabric width. If you prefer, you may repurpose old jeans. Make sure you are able to cut a total of (42) 10" squares as well as (168) 3" squares.

**NOTE: If you are using the same black denim for both the 3" squares and the border, the yardage can be combined. You will need 1¾ yards if you make that choice.

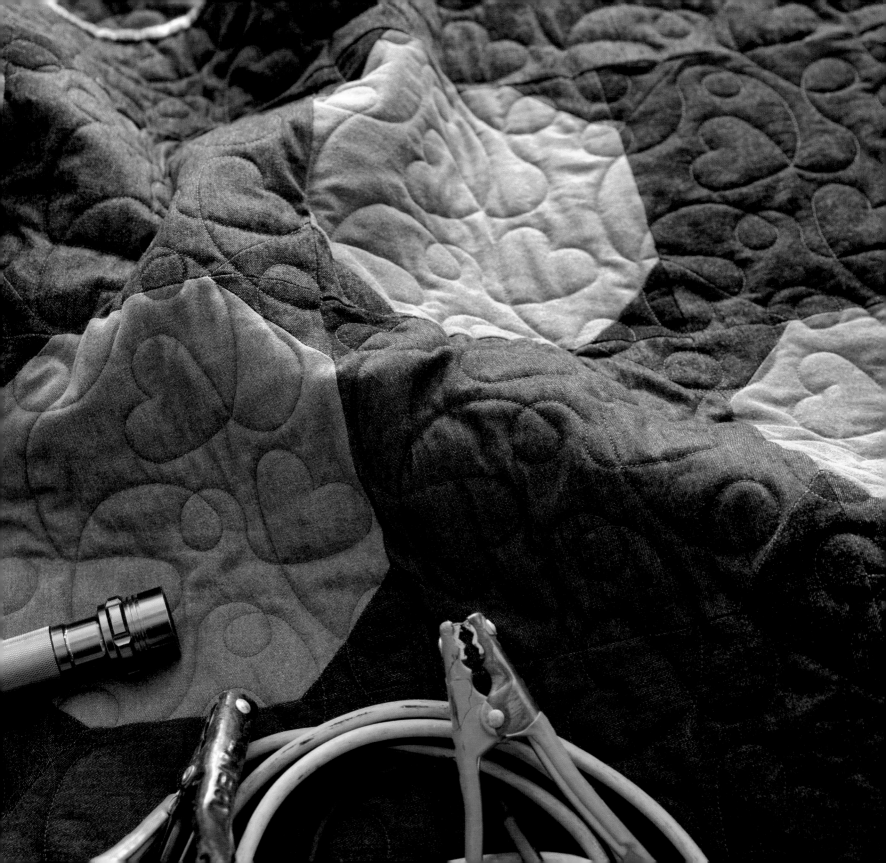

1 cut

From the light blue denim, cut:

(4) 10" strips across the width of the fabric – subcut 3 strips into 10" squares. Cut (1) 10" square from the remaining strip. Each strip will yield 5 squares and a **total of 16** squares are needed. Set the remainder of the last strip aside for another project.

From the dark blue denim, cut:

(6) 10" strips across the width of the fabric – subcut 5 strips into 10" squares. Cut (1) 10" square from the remaining strip. Each strip will yield 5 squares and a total of 26 squares are needed. Set the remainder of the last strip aside for another project.

From the black denim, cut:

(10) 3" strips across the width of the fabric – subcut 9 strips into 3" squares. Cut (6) 3" squares from the remaining strip. Each strip will yield 18 squares and a **total of 168** are needed. Set the remainder of the last strip aside for another project. If you used yardage rather than repurposed jeans, set aside the remainder of the fabric for the border.

2 make snowballed blocks

On the reverse side of each of the (168) 3" black denim squares, draw a line from corner to corner once on the diagonal. To snowball the first corner of the square, place a marked square atop a corner of a 10" square with right sides facing. Sew on the marked line. Trim the excess fabric away ¼" from the sewn seam. Open and press the seam allowance toward the dark fabric. Repeat to snowball the remaining 3 corners. **2A**

Make 16 light blue blocks and 26 dark blue blocks for a **total of 42** blocks.

Block Size: 9½" finished

2A

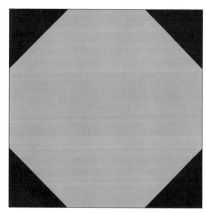

3 arrange and sew

Lay out the blocks in rows. Each row is made up of **6 blocks** across and **7 rows** are needed. Press the seam allowances of the even rows toward the right and the odd rows toward the left to make the seams nest. Sew the rows together to complete the center of the quilt. Refer to the diagram on page 79 for color placement.

4 border

Cut (5) 6″ strips across the width of the fabric. Sew the strips together end-to-end to make one long strip. Trim the borders from this strip.

Refer to Borders (pg. 118) in the Construction Basics to measure and cut the outer borders. The strips are approximately 67″ for the sides and approximately 68½″ for the top and bottom.

5 quilt and bind

Layer the quilt with batting and backing and quilt. After the quilting is complete, square up the quilt and trim away all excess batting and backing. Add binding to complete the quilt. See Construction Basics (pg. 118) for binding instructions.

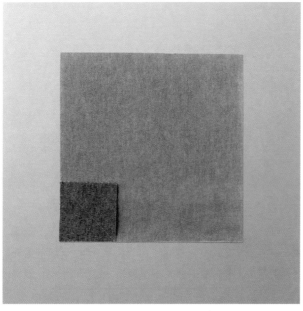

1 Draw a line from corner to corner once on the diagonal on the reverse side of the 3″ black denim squares. Place 1 square on one corner of a 10″ square with right sides facing. Sew on the marked line.

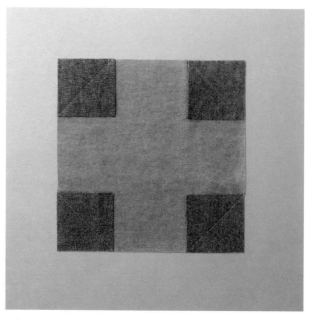

2 Repeat for all 4 corners of the 10″ square.

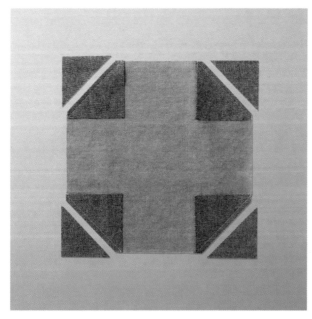

3 Trim the excess fabric away ¼″ from the sewn seam line.

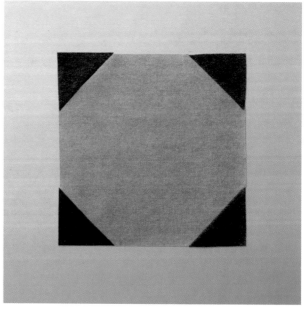

4 Open each corner and press to complete 1 snowballed block.

For the tutorial and everything you need to make this quilt visit:
www.msqc.co/celebrateblock19

all stars

We have a strong tradition of military service in our small town. Many families have loved ones in the armed services and we're so grateful for their sacrifices to protect our homeland. Just a few years ago, the number of families who were separated by military deployment was over a million. Thankfully, those numbers have dropped, but for families who continue to serve, the key to staying strong while they're separated is good communication.

I spoke with two couples who have spent time apart and I gained a whole new appreciation for the little traditions that families have. Each had simple, unique ways of staying in touch and showing love for each other.

Becky and Aaron were married just after he joined the National Guard. Becky said, "I didn't consider how his choice would affect my life. It was supposed to be one weekend a month and two weeks out of the year. Little did I know that September 11th was right around the corner." Soon after that, he was deployed to remote places like Kosovo, Afghanistan, Germany, and Ukraine.

At one point, they spent two years apart, with only occasional phone calls, emails, and a few care packages to keep in touch. Becky said, "Fortunately, technology has changed a lot and now we can chat daily rather than waiting weeks to communicate." They also have two xBox systems that allow Aaron to play games online with their kids while he's away.

Karie and Dain were separated for 8 months while he was in Warrant Officer Basic School. She said they were able to keep in touch via Skype, letters, email, text, and phone.

He also prerecorded the kids' favorite bedtime stories. On Sundays, he even ate dinner with them via Facetime at his spot at the table!

Reunions are the sweetest part for these families. They go to the airport to pick up their husbands, complete with signs and balloons. Karie said that her kids make signs that say things like, "Welcome home, Daddy! You're finally home!" and cry with joy when they see him. Becky said, "The reunions are great! But they can also be very hard. They say a deployment can make or break a relationship, and that holds true. Being patient with one another and allowing time for adjustment is imperative." The best part about homecoming, she says, is, "The first hug. That first kiss. Seeing them and remembering every facial feature that may have faded from your mind over time. Not worrying about their safety. Watching him interact with your kids. Not being alone every night. Not carrying the burden of holding everything together when all you want to do is cry."

Although deployment can be tough, it has strengthened their families by helping them to treasure the time they have together. Finally, Becky said, "Deployments are certainly not for the weak! While I didn't see myself as a 'military wife' when we got married, I've learned the ropes over the past 17 years. If you have family or friends experiencing a deployed spouse, find ways to help them. Being the spouse of a servicemember is an honor, and I'm proud of my husband, but having a support system that strengthens me while he's gone is key to my survival."

materials

QUILT SIZE
62½" x 72"

BLOCK SIZE
9½" finished

QUILT TOP
1 package of 10" print squares
1¾ yards navy or contrasting solid
   of your choice

BORDER
¾ yard

BINDING
¾ yard

BACKING
4½ yards - vertical seam(s)

SAMPLE QUILT
American Valor by Stephanie
Marrott for Wilmington Prints

2A

1 cut

From navy fabric cut:

- (21) 2½" strips across the width of the fabric - subcut each strip into 2½" x 5" rectangles. Each strip will yield 8 rectangles and a **total of 168** are needed.

2 sew

Place a 2½" navy rectangle atop 1 corner of a 10" print square on an angle with right sides facing. Position the rectangle so it will cover the corner once it has been pressed down. Sew in place and press toward the outside edge of the block. **2A 2B**

Turn the block over so the reverse side is showing. Trim the excess fabric away evenly with the edge of the background square. **2C 2D**

Place the next rectangle on the next corner. Follow the directions above and stitch in place as before. Repeat for all 4 corners to complete 1 block. Notice

how all the narrow, pointed pieces are going in the same direction. **Make 42. 2E**

Block Size: 9½" finished.

3 cut

Select 11 blocks. Cut each in half to make 5" x 10" rectangles. Set aside for the moment. **3A**

Select 1 block and cut it in half vertically and horizontally to make (4) 5" squares. Set aside while you lay out the quilt. **3B**

4 arrange and sew

Lay out the blocks in rows. Each row is made up of 5 whole blocks and has a half block (5" x 10" rectangle) on each end. Lay out **6 rows** and sew them together. **4A**

2B

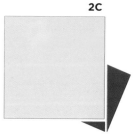

2C

2D

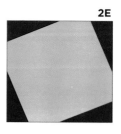

2E

3A

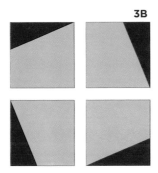

3B

4A

4B

Make **2 rows** using 5 half-blocks and 2 quarter blocks. Place the quarter blocks on each end of the rows. Notice how each star along the edge of the quilt is complete with all 4 points in place. **4B**

Sew the rows together to complete the center of the quilt.

5 border

Cut (7) 3½" strips across the width of the fabric. Sew the strips together end-to-end to make one long strip. Trim the borders from this strip.

Refer to Borders (pg. 118) in the Construction Basics to measure and cut the outer borders. The strips are approximately 66½" for the sides and approximately 63" for the top and bottom.

6 quilt and bind

Layer the quilt with batting and backing and quilt. After the quilting is complete, square up the quilt and trim away all excess batting and backing. Add binding to complete the quilt. See Construction Basics (pg. 118) for binding instructions.

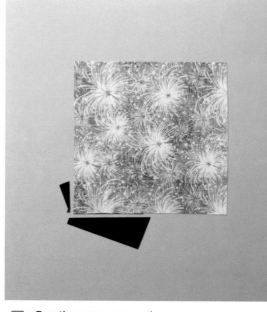

1 Position a 2½" x 5" rectangle atop 1 corner of a 10" print square on an angle with right sides facing. Sew in place.

2 Press the sewn rectangle toward the outside edge of the square.

3 Turn the square over so the reverse side is showing. Trim the excess fabric away evenly with the edge of the print square.

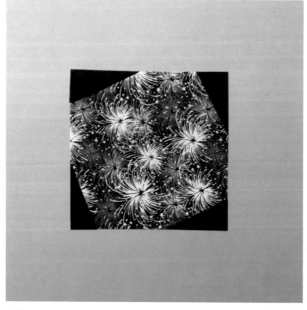

4 After trimming the excess fabric away, press the star point toward the outer edge of the square.

5 Repeat for all 4 corners of the square to complete 1 block. Notice that all the narrow, pointed pieces are going the same direction around the square.

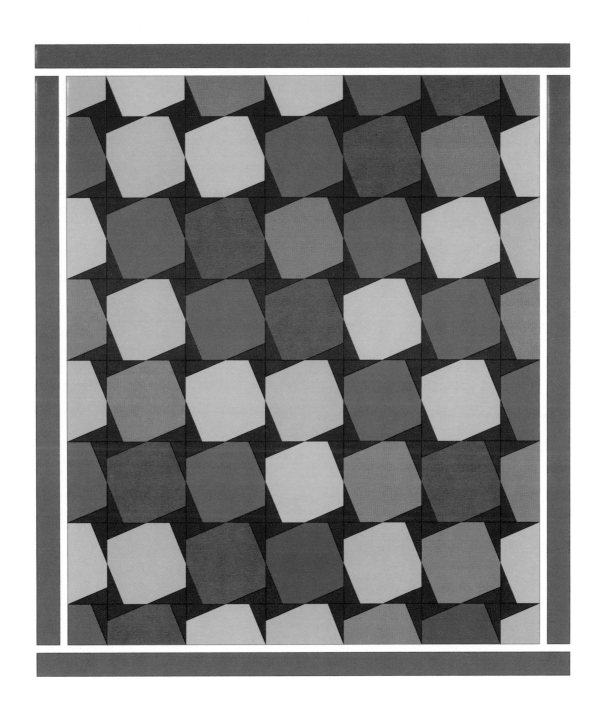

celebrate good times!

five quick celebration projects for any occasion

These sweet handmade gifts come together in a snap and don't take months to create. They're customizable for any occasion and definitely show you care. From cute aprons and table runners to T-shirt wall hangings and darling denim baskets, plus a sweet ring bearer pillow that's the perfect finishing touch for the next wedding, it's easy to make something from the heart.

Special occasions have a tendency to sneak up on us! It always seems like there's so much time to prepare, but when the date gets closer, the time for preparation soon runs out. Believe me, I have been caught unawares with a wedding only a week or two away, wondering what I might give to the bride and groom! But, before you regift that Crock Pot, take a moment to make something they're sure to treasure.

A quilt is a nice idea, but can create a stressful situation when it isn't ready on time. I remember a young lady expressing her lament that she showed up to her sister's wedding with only the promise of a wedding quilt, and while the couple was gracious, she wished she could have brought something that day for them and gifted them the quilt later. Why not a matching pair of aprons for the newlyweds? It would be a nice touch with a set of kitchen utensils!

And birthdays do come around once a year, but it can be hard to remember them at times. Thank goodness Facebook reminds us, but without much time to spare.

What to do? Well, I think a fast and fabulous table runner to match the birthday decor would be lovely!

When you send your child off to school, don't just throw away their old jeans. Create a cute set of denim bowls to help keep the dorm room clutter in check! A set of matching pillows would also go a long way to making it feel like home.

But what about the guy who has everything? I bet he doesn't have a wonderfully thoughtful T-shirt wall hanging! My guess is, just about everyone has a stack of T-shirts that doesn't quite fit anymore, but are filled with fond memories. The next time he cleans out his closet, sneak in and take that stack of discarded shirts and whip up a handmade item that's sure to impress!

Just because a gift doesn't take a lot of time to make, doesn't mean it isn't thoughtful. We all have busy lives and do our best to be generous with the time we have. None of these gifts take more than an afternoon and they equal big smiles, believe me! Sometimes the best gifts are the simplest ones.

all-purpose apron

supplies

ADULT-SIZE APRON SUPPLY LIST

1 yard for apron skirt and waistband/ties

¼ yard coordinating fabric for pocket

CHILD-SIZE APRON SUPPLY LIST

½ yard for apron skirt and waistband/ties

¼ yard coordinating fabric for pocket

---

1 cut

Adult-Sized Apron

From the 1 yard, cut:

- (1) 40" x 16" for body of apron

- (3) 5" x width of fabric strips for waistband/ties

From the ¼ yard, cut:

- (1) 40" x 9" for pocket

Child-Sized Apron

From the ½ yard, cut:

- (1) 21" x 8½" for body of apron

- (2) 4½" x width of fabric strips for waistband/ties

From the ¼ yard, cut:

- (1) 21" x 5" for pocket

2 sew

Note: Instructions for adult-sized and child-sized aprons are the same. The dimensions for both sizes are written in the pattern.

Fold one of the long edges of the pocket ¼" toward the wrong side of the fabric, then press. Fold an additional ¼" and press again to enclose raw edges. Topstitch along the folded edge to create the top of the pocket.

With the right side of the pocket and the wrong side of the apron skirt facing, line the bottom edge of the pocket up with the bottom edge of the apron. Sew across the bottom edge to attach the 2 pieces. Bring the pocket around to the front and press. **2A**

Fold the apron in half, press, and mark the center of the pocket.

with a fabric pen. Then measure 10″ for the adult size or 5″ for the child size on either side of the center and mark those lines. Sew on all 3 lines to create the pockets, backstitching at the beginning and end of the seams to secure stitches. **2B**

Fold the 2 sides of the apron ¼″ toward the wrong side of the fabric, then press. Fold an additional ¼″ and press again to enclose raw edges. Stitch down each side of the apron to secure the pocket.

Leaving 4″- 6″ thread tails at the beginning and end, sew a basting stitch ¼″ from the top edge of the apron. Do not backstitch at either end. Repeat and sew a second row of basting stitches ¼″ from the previous row. Holding the bobbin thread tails firmly, begin to gather the fabric from one side toward the center. Repeat the gathering, working from the other side into the center. When the top edge of the apron measures 28″ for the adult size or 16″ for the

child size, knot the thread tails on each side to hold the gathers in place. Adjust the gathers, evenly spacing them to your liking. **2C**

Sew the strips cut for the waistband/ ties together end-to-end to create one long strip. If making a child sized apron, trim the strip to 59″. Fold and press all 4 edges under ¼″ to enclose raw edges. Fold waistband in half lengthwise and press.

Mark the center of the waistband and apron skirt. Line up the center of both pieces and insert top edge of apron skirt into folded edge of waistband. Pin in place. Stitch down one side, then along the bottom, and up the other side of the waistband to attach the 2 pieces. Repeat a second row of stitching for added durability. **2D**

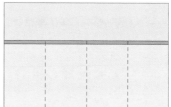

2A

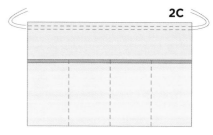

2B

2C

2D

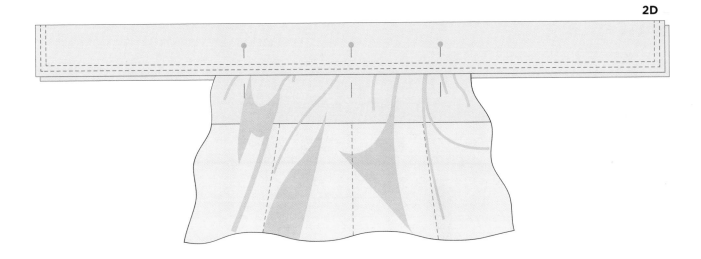

t-shirt wall hanging

size: 24″ x 24″
block size: 24″ finished

supplies

1 T-shirt
(4) 7″ print squares
½ yard background fabric
13″ square Heat n Bond Fusible Interfacing – medium weight
¼ yard binding fabric
1 yard backing fabric

1 cut

From the background fabric, cut:

* (1) 7″ strip across the width of the fabric – subcut (4) 7″ squares from the strip.

* (1) 6½″ strip across the width of the fabric – subcut (4) 6½″ squares from the strip.

2 prepare t-shirt

Wash and dry the shirt you have chosen. Trim off the neckband, the sleeves and the hem. Cut the front of the shirt away from the back, leaving as wide a margin as possible on either side of the portion of the shirt you would like to feature. Keep in mind that we will be trimming the featured portion to a 12½″ square, so make sure it will fit in that measurement.

Cut a 13″ square of fusible interfacing. Center it on top of the reverse side of the portion of the shirt you want to feature. Adhere the fusible to the reverse side of the shirt following the manufacturer's instructions. Once the fusible is bonded to the shirt, trim the featured portion to a 12½″ square. Set aside for the moment.

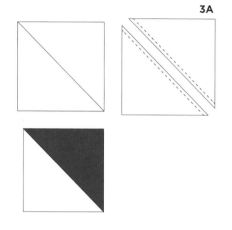

3A

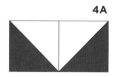

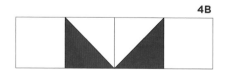

4A

4B

3 make half-square triangles

On the reverse side of the (4) 7″ background squares, draw a line from corner to corner once on the diagonal. Layer a marked background square with a 7″ print square. Sew on both sides of the drawn line using a ¼″ seam allowance. Cut on the line and open each half-square triangle unit. Press the seam allowance toward the dark fabric. Repeat, using the remaining 7″ squares. Each of the sewn squares will yield 2 half-square triangle units and a **total of 8** are needed. Square up each unit to 6½″. **3A**

4 block construction

Make paired half-square triangle units by sewing 2 units together as shown. **Make 4. 4A**

Sew a 6½″ background square to both ends of a paired half-square triangle unit to make the top and bottom rows. **4B**

Sew a paired half-square triangle unit to both sides of the 12½″ T-shirt square to make the center row. **4C**

Sew the 3 rows together to complete the block. **4D**

Block Size: 24″ finished

5 quilt and bind

Layer the wall hanging with batting and backing and quilt. After the quilting is complete, square up the wall hanging and trim away all excess batting and backing. Add binding to complete the wall hanging.

4C

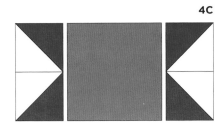

4D

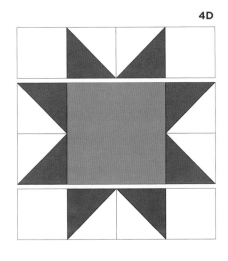

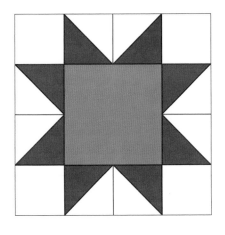

denim basket

supplies
A pair of jeans
1 fat quarter for the lining

1 cutting instructions

From the denim, cut:
- (1) 12" piece near the bottom of the leg **1A**

From the fat quarter, cut:
- (2) pieces, 12" length x the width of the denim, plus 1"

2 create the lining

Note: Use a ½" seam allowance for this entire project.

With right sides together, join the 2 lining pieces by stitching down both sides. Sew across the bottom of the lining, leaving a 4" gap for turning. **2A** Make boxed corners by pulling on one corner of the bag until a peak is formed. Measure 1½" from the point of the peak and draw a line straight across. Sew on the drawn line, then trim the excess fabric away ½" from the sewn seam. Repeat for the other corner. **2B**

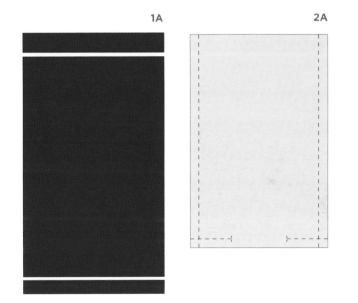

1A

2A

3 create the outer layer

Turn your denim piece wrong side out. Sew all the way across the bottom edge.

Follow the directions in section 2 to make boxed corners on the denim piece. Turn the denim piece right side out.

4 complete the basket

Insert the denim piece inside of the lining, with right sides together. Line up the boxed corners and the top edge of both pieces. Once everything is in place, pin around the top edge if desired. **4A**

Join the 2 pieces by sewing around the top edge.

Turn the entire unit right side out, using the opening in the lining. After turning, topstitch the opening in the lining closed. Tuck the lining inside the denim.

Press around the top edge and topstitch to complete the basket. Fold the top over as desired and enjoy! **4B**

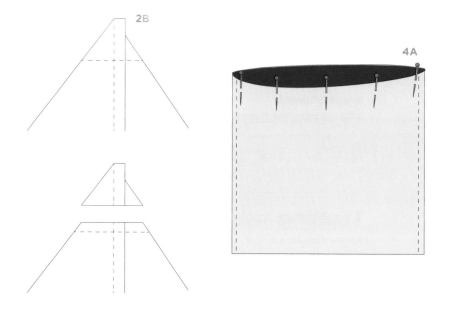

3D pinwheel table runner

size: 13" x 31"
block size: 9" finished

supplies
1 package 5" squares
¼ yard for binding
½ yard for backing

1 fold and sew
Fold a dark square from corner to corner once on the diagonal and press the crease in place. Place the folded square onto the upper right corner of a light background square. Align the raw edges of the folded piece with the raw edges of the background square. **1A**

Begin at the top and sew down the right side, using a ⅛" seam allowance. (We want this seam allowance to be smaller than usual.) **1B**

Fold the loose corner of the folded triangle toward the sewn seam on the right. Pin in place. Turn so the folded portion is on the right and sew down that side of the block using a ⅛" seam allowance. This completes one quadrant of the block. **Make 4 quadrants. 1C**

Using a ¼" seam allowance, sew the 4 quadrants together as shown to complete 1 block. **Make 3. 1D**

Sew the 3 blocks together to complete the center of the table runner.

2 border
Cut:
• (8) 5" squares in half to make (16) 2½" x 5" rectangles.
• (1) 5" square in fourths to make (4) 2½" squares.

3 sew
Sew (6) 2½" x 5" rectangles together to make a top and bottom border. **Make 2** and sew one to the top and bottom of the table runner.

Sew (2) 2½" x 5" rectangles together. Add a 2½" square to each end of the strip. **Make 2** and sew one to either side of the table runner. **3A**

4 quilt and bind
Layer the table runner with batting and backing and quilt. After the quilting is complete, square it up and trim away all excess batting and backing. Add binding to complete the table runner.

1A 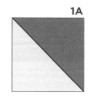 **1B** **1C**

1D

3A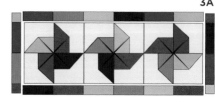

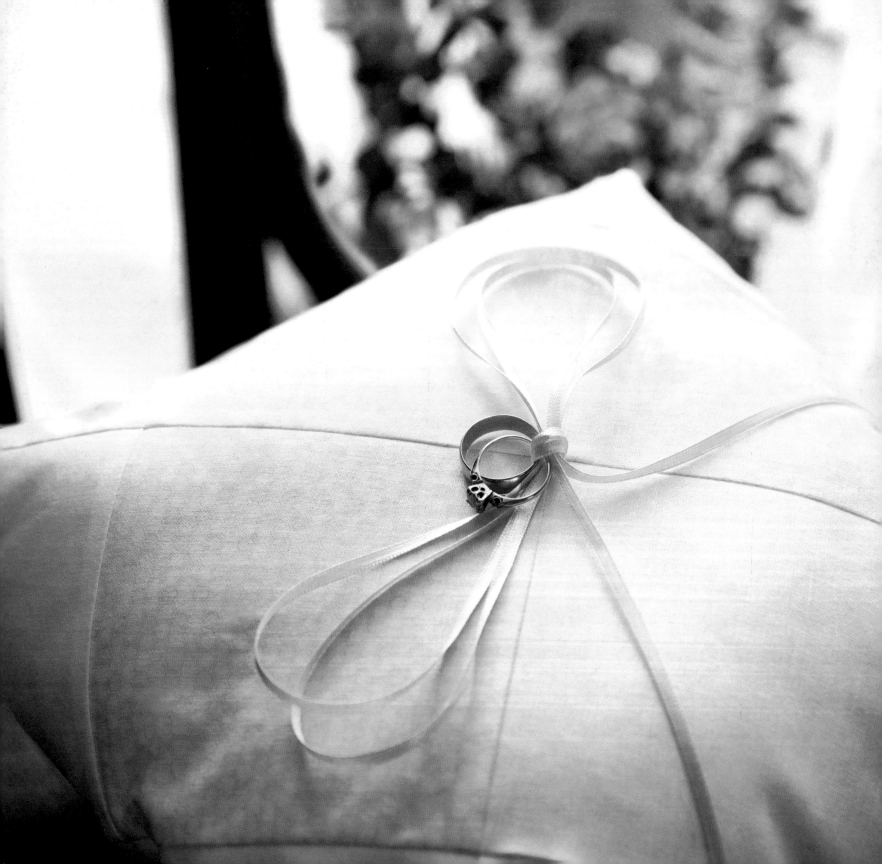

ring bearer's pillow

size: 13" x 13"

supplies
(16) 5" squares
2 yards ¼" wide satin ribbon
Poly-Fil Fiber

arrange and sew

Arrange the squares in a 4 x 4 grid. The middle 4 squares will be the center of the pillow. Sew the squares into 4 rows using a ¼" seam allowance. Press the seam allowances of the first and third rows toward the right and the seams of the second and fourth rows toward the left. Sew the rows together to make an 18½" square. **1A**

Fold the 18½" square in half with right sides together. Stitch the short ends closed. **1B 1C**

Bring the 2 side seams you just stitched together and match them up. Stitch the open seam together beginning at 1 end. Sew part way up, and backstitch. Remove the pillow from under the sewing machine foot. Turn the pillow and start sewing the open seam closed from the other end. Stop when you have an opening that is about 4" and backstitch. **1D**

Turn the pillow right side out and fill with the Poly-Fil fiber. Once it is filled to your satisfaction, sew the opening closed using a ladder stitch or a whipstitch.

Fold the length of ribbon in half. Position it on the center seam of the pillow and stitch in place on the fold.

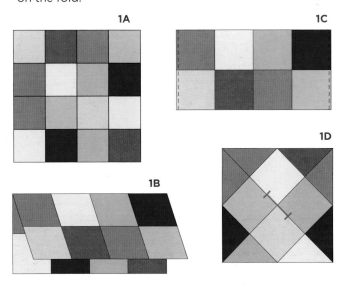

1A

1C

1B

1D

REFERENCE

all stars

QUILT SIZE
62½" x 72"

BLOCK SIZE
9½" finished

QUILT TOP
1 package of 10" print squares
1¾ yards navy or contrasting solid
 of your choice

BORDER
¾ yard

BINDING
¾ yard

BACKING
4½ yards - vertical seam(s)

SAMPLE QUILT
American Valor by Stephanie
Marrott for Wilmington Prints

QUILTING PATTERN
Simple Stipple

ONLINE TUTORIALS
msqc.co/celebrateblock19

PATTERN
pg. 80

crown jewel

QUILT SIZE
77" x 77"

BLOCK SIZE
16" finished

QUILT TOP
3½ yards black fabric - includes
    outer border
2¾ yards of background fabric - includes
    inner border
1¼ yards of gold or complementary
    fabric of your choice

BINDING
¾ yard

BACKING
5 yards - vertical seam(s) or 2½ yards
    of 108" wide

SAMPLE QUILT
Bella Solids Golden Wheat, Bella Solids
Black

QUILTING PATTERN
Back to School

ONLINE TUTORIALS
msqc.co/celebrateblock19

PATTERN
pg. 40

attic windows panel

QUILT SIZE
65" x 43¼"

BLOCK SIZE
9½" x 10¾" finished

QUILT TOP
(1) 42" x 28" panel
½ yard white fabric
1¼ yards tan fabric – includes
  outer border
¾ yard black fabric – includes
  inner border

BINDING
½ yard

BACKING
3 yards - vertical seam(s)

SAMPLE QUILT
High Ridge Crossing by Terry
Doughty for Northcott Fabrics

QUILTING PATTERN
Simple Stipple

ONLINE TUTORIALS
msqc.co/celebrateblock19

PATTERN
pg. 48

denim snowball quilt

QUILT SIZE
68" x 77½"

BLOCK SIZE
9½" finished

QUILT TOP*
1¼ yards light blue denim
1¾ yards dark blue denim
1 yard black denim**

BORDER
1 yard**

BINDING
½ yard

BACKING
4¾ yards - vertical seam(s)

SAMPLE QUILT
Indigo Denim by Robert Kaufman Fabrics

QUILTING PATTERN
Heart Large

ONLINE TUTORIALS
msqc.co/celebrateblock19

PATTERN
pg. 72

*NOTE: The yardage for this quilt is based on 56" useable fabric width. If you prefer, you may repurpose old jeans. Make sure you are able to cut a total of (42) 10" squares as well as (168) 3" squares.

**NOTE: If you are using the same black denim for both the 3" squares and the border, the yardage can be combined. You will need 1¾ yards if you make that choice.

diamond dance

QUILT SIZE
90" x 88"

BLOCK SIZE
4⅛" x 9½" finished

QUILT TOP
1 package 10" print fabric
3 yards background squares -
 includes inner border
1½ yards complementary fabric

OUTER BORDER
1½ yards

BINDING
¾ yard

BACKING
8 yards - vertical seam(s) or 2¾
 yards of 108" wide

OTHER
Missouri Star 10" Half-Hexagon
 Template
Missouri Star Large Rhombus
 Template

SAMPLE QUILT
Seventh Inning Stretch by Jennifer
Pugh for Wilmington Prints

QUILTING PATTERN
Baseball Stars

ONLINE TUTORIALS
msqc.co/celebrateblock19

PATTERN
pg. 16

disappearing double pinwheel

QUILT SIZE
81" x 92"

BLOCK SIZE
11" finished

QUILT TOP
1 package of 10" print squares
1 package of 10" background squares

INNER BORDER
¾ yard

OUTER BORDER
1¾ yards

BINDING
¾ yard

BACKING
8½ yards - vertical seam(s) or 2¾ yards
   108" wide

SAMPLE QUILT
Bed of Roses by Edyta Sitar for
   Andover Fabrics

QUILTING PATTERN
Arc Doodle

ONLINE TUTORIALS
msqc.co/celebrateblock19

PATTERN
pg. 56

periwinkle
on point

QUILT SIZE
71" x 71"

BLOCK SIZE
7" finished

QUILT TOP
4 packages of 5" print squares
3¾ yards of background fabric -
    includes inner border

OUTER BORDER
1¼ yards

BINDING
¾ yard

BACKING
4½ yards - vertical seam(s)

OTHER SUPPLIES
Lapel Stick (glue stick)
2 packages Mini Wacky Web
    Triangle Papers
Missouri Star Quilt Co. - Mini
    Periwinkle(Wacky Web) Template

SAMPLE QUILT
Big Bang by Deborah Edwards for
Northcott

QUILTING PATTERN
Champagne Bubbles

ONLINE TUTORIALS
msqc.co/celebrateblock19

PATTERN
pg. 64

radiance

QUILT SIZE
70" x 70"

BLOCK SIZE
9½" finished

QUILT TOP
1 roll of 2½" print strips
1 package of 10" background squares

INNER BORDER
½ yard

BINDING
¾ yard

BACKING
4½ yards - vertical seam(s)

OTHER SUPPLIES
Missouri Star Quilt Co.-
    Burst Block Template

SAMPLE QUILT
Porcelain by 3 Sisters for Moda
Fabrics

QUILTING PATTERN
Debs Feathers

ONLINE TUTORIALS
msqc.co/celebrateblock19

PATTERN
pg. 32

rose
garden

QUILT SIZE
67½" x 67½"

BLOCK SIZE
4½" finished

QUILT TOP
2 packages of 5" print squares
1½ yards of pink fabric
1¼ yards of white fabric

BORDER
1¼ yards

BINDING
¾ yard

BACKING
4¼ yards - vertical seam(s)

OTHER SUPPLIES
Clearly Perfect Slotted Trimmer B

SAMPLE QUILT
Best Friends Forever by Stacy Iest
Hsu for Moda Fabrics

QUILTING PATTERN
Simple Stipple

ONLINE TUTORIALS
msqc.co/celebrateblock19

PATTERN
pg. 8

t-shirt quilt

QUILT SIZE
68½" x 83"

BLOCK SIZE
12" finished

QUILT TOP
20 T-shirts
1½ yards white fabric – includes
    inner border
½ yard print fabric

OUTER BORDER
1¼ yards

BINDING
¾ yard

BACKING
5 yards - vertical seam(s)

OTHER SUPPLIES
7½ yards Medium Weight Fusible
    Interfacing

SAMPLE QUILT
Simply Happy by Dodi Poulson for
Riley Blake Designs (Outer Border),
Hopscotch - Rose Petals Nosegay by
Jamie Fingal for RJR Fabrics

QUILTING PATTERN
Curly Twirly Flowers

ONLINE TUTORIALS
msqc.co/celebrateblock19

PATTERN
pg. 24

construction basics

general quilting

- All seams are ¼" unless directions specify differently.
- Precuts are not prewashed; so do not prewash other fabrics in the project.
- Remove all selvages.

press seams

- Set the temperature of the iron on the cotton setting.
- Set the seam by pressing it just as it was sewn, right sides together.
- Place the darker fabric on top, lift, and press back.
- Press seam allowances toward the borders unless directed otherwise.

borders

- Always measure the quilt top in 3 different places vertically before cutting side borders.
- Start measuring about 4" in from the top and bottom.
- Take the average of those 3 measurements.
- Cut 2 border strips to that size. Piece strips together if needed.
- Attach one to either side of the quilt. Position the border fabric on top as you sew to prevent waviness and to keep the quilt straight.
- Repeat this process for the top and bottom borders, measuring the width 3 times. Include the newly attached side borders in your measurements.

backing

- Measure the quilt top vertically and horizontally. Add 8" to both measurements to make sure you have an extra 4" all the way around to make allowance for the fabric that is taken up in the quilting process as well as having adequate fabric for the quilting frame.
- Trim off all selvages and use a ½" seam allowance when piecing the backing. Sew the pieces together along the longest edge. Press the seam allowance open to decrease bulk.
- Use horizontal seams for smaller quilts (under 60" wide), vertical seams for larger quilts.
- Don't hesitate to cut a length of fabric in half along the fold line if it means saving fabric and makes the quilt easier to handle.
- Choose a backing layout that best suits your quilt. Note: large quilts might require 3 lengths.

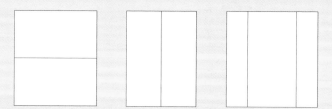

binding

find a video tutorial at: www.msqc.co/006

- Use 2½" strips for binding.
- Sew strips together end-to-end into one long strip using diagonal seams, a.k.a. plus sign method (next). Press seams open.
- Fold in half lengthwise with wrong sides together and press.
- The entire length should equal the outside dimension of the quilt plus 15" - 20".